HORSE WOMAN

PRAISE FOR HORSE WOMAN

"Lee's voice conveys something that all of us horsewomen know, that a horse is not just a horse, but the embodiment of our hopes, dreams, fears, failures and accomplishments. I am a student of her work and grateful to call her a friend."

– *Vanessa Mannix, Canadian Equestrian Team Member*

"Full of wit and wisdom, equine and people truths, this is a must-read, must-use book. Highly recommended, it will definitely be part of my tack room collection."

– *Julie Moorcroft, 2016 World Champion, Western Dressage*

"A fabulous book, giving us real insight into the extraordinary life of a true horsewoman."

– *Susan Oakes, World Record Holder in Sidesaddle High Jumping*

"Part Will Rogers, part Emily Post, Lee has the uncanny ability to share from the horse's perspective. She inspires us to be more aware and in tune with our horse partners … and quite possibly, to be better people because of it."

– *Gary Rempel, Canadian Finals Rodeo and Wrangler National Finals Rodeo Pickup Man*

"The importance of mentors and continual learning throughout Lee's book struck true to me. This is a must in my world. It is important to watch and listen to other horsemen and women … and to learn from each horse we have the honour to step across."

– *John Swales, 2017 National Reined Cow Horse Association World's Greatest Horseman*

"Lee McLean is a friend and colleague who I consider to be one of the most knowledgeable women in the horse world today. She is authentic and common sense prevails, as you will come to understand, while reading Horse Woman."

– *Cub Wright, 2008 Canadian Open Cutting Champion*

"Lee doesn't just offer practical advice in Horse Woman. She takes her readers inside the minds of those who pursue deeper understanding of the animals they love. This book is destined to become a classic. I wish I'd had a copy when I was a girl … It's a comfort, like having a friend talking to you, saying what you're maybe too embarrassed, or to unsure, to ask."

– *Adrian 'Buckaroogirl' Brannan, Author and Singer-Songwriter*

"Bound within these pages, Lee's knowledge and experience gathered over a lifetime is a must-read for anyone interested in the life of a deeply-rooted horse woman. Delivered in her own brilliant style of storytelling, infused with decades of wisdom, the authenticity of this book is a complete refresh in the digital world today."

– *Shannon Lawlor, Equine Artist*

"Insightful, witty, heartfelt and filled with nuggets of horsemanship advice garnered from plenty of wet saddle blankets. This Horse Woman will quickly become the friend you want to share a pot of coffee with and chat horses all day."

– *Robyn Duplisea, Publisher, Show Horse Today*

"There are many books about the art of riding or the bond between equines and humans, but perhaps none are so passionately written. A vivid storyteller and a keeper of western heritage, this Horse Woman offers hope to the rest of us who, like so many others, can find ourselves intimidated by horses and the culture with which they are aligned."

– *Jenn Webster, Publisher, Western Horse Review*

RED BARN BOOKS
CARSTAIRS, ALBERTA, CANADA
REDBARNBOOKS.CA

TEXT © LEE MCLEAN 2019

All rights reserved. No part of this book may be reproduced or copied in any form, or by any means, without written consent from the publisher.

BOOK DESIGN: LIA GOLEMBA | PINK SPOT STUDIOS
FRONT COVER IMAGE: TARA MCKENZIE
BACK COVER IMAGE: NOAH FALLIS

#HORSEWOMAN
To book a talk, bookstore visit, or book club Q&A,

EMAIL
INFO@REDBARNBOOKS.CA

TRADE EDITION
978-1-9991087-5-5

HORSE WOMAN
*Notes on Living Well
& Riding Better*

LEE M^CLEAN
*Author of the acclaimed
Keystone Equine blog*

SAFETY DISCLAIMER

Please note that by taking part in horsemanship or any of the suggestions herein, you are agreeing to not hold liable Lee McLean, her family, Keystone Equine, Red Barn Books, or employees thereof, should any misfortune occur as a result of your training or actions.

We recommend that you seek the help of a professional and use an approved helmet and correct riding footwear when working with any pony or horse. Archival photos used in this book may predate modern safety standards. The content herein is anecdotal. Your own common sense and safety must be uppermost. Horses can be dangerous, handle them at your own risk.

ACKNOWLEDGEMENTS

In my words are the memory of so many voices. Dad, Wendy and Hank Rudosky, Bill Gow, Shirley Van Leeuwen, Michael Khan, E.M. Boerschmann, Vance Kaglea. Thank you all.

Mum and Kerry, bless you for being soft on my feelings but holding firm on the multitude of 'three little dots'. Ayesha and Lia of Red Barn Books, thank you for offering me shelter. I am indebted to every one of my readers for giving me the courage to write.

Most of all, I give thanks to Mike, my family and to my horses. These stories belong to them.

CONTENTS

INTRODUCTION

WINTER: HOPE

Great Expectations	6
Too Cold to Ride	20
Saddle Up	35

SPRING: WELLNESS

Mentorship	58
A Time to Heal	72
Blessings	88

SUMMER: LEARNING

It's a Good Life… If You Don't Weaken	114
It's Showtime	127
Back to School	139

AUTUMN: REFLECTION

Happy Trails	164
Remembrance	177
'Tis the Season	192

CONCLUSION

BOOK CLUB QUESTIONS

INDEX

INTRODUCTION

Where did this journey start?

While I always loved horses, or more rightly the idea of horses, I was sent to the hospital after a hard fall from a pony at the age of four. I still have the scar on my chin, a reminder that the love and courage possessed by young children is precious. Difficult to replace, this invincible spirit needs to be kept safe.

At the time that I was starting school, I kept Walter Farley's beloved book, *Little Black, A Pony,* at my bedside. In an unusual twist, the small pony was the hero of the story, doing something that Big Red, the beautiful horse, could not. Afraid to ride but still wanting to, I fell hard in love with Little Black.

When I was six, I went with my father to an auction sale held just outside of town. The barn was well-known to me, a place where shadowy men did horse deals by the lights of their pickup trucks. Arguments were solved with the brandishing of knives and the local police were often there, asking questions. Still, this a place where I somehow felt at home.

The day of the auction was very cold. Frozen sap of the jack-pines cracked like gunshots. I had a fur-trimmed hood on my parka and wore new sealskin boots. I remember this because my clothing, along with my small stature, caused a great commotion among the assembled sale horses. Many of the local ranchers added to their winter income by chasing and capturing wild horses in the bush. Most of these had been run into the corrals only the day previously.

Few of the horses in the pole corrals, judging by their frosty snorts and restless movement, appeared to be broke. Except one. She was a black pony with such a hair coat that she appeared truly round. She had four white feet and these were festooned with balls of ice as she walked up to me and nuzzled, first my parka hood, then my fur boots. She picked me out before I picked her. It was love at first sight.

One of the old ranchers showed me that the black pony was broke because when he pulled on her forelock, she gave with her head and led right alongside him. I tried it myself and excitedly called to my father.

"Dad, the black pony!" I kept suggesting but my father was not one to brook childish interruptions.

He was talking business amid much loud laughter. My dreams for the pony didn't stand a chance. Watching the auction through the bars of the corrals, I stood silently while the pony entered the ring and was sold. I knew that my father had not even put in a bid.

I was spending a rare good day in the cold, with these men and horses. I tried to be happy. The day passed and the men, one by one, left to start their trucks and head home. As Dad and I were leaving, we were approached by one of my father's old friends. Quietly, with a wink for me and a handshake for my father, he handed us a bill of sale written out on the back of a Christmas card.

"Sold for full value received, one black Shetland mare with four white feet. Signed, Hank Rudosky." I have the 'document' still. With that, my father wrote out a cheque in the amount of $27.50 for the pony that would change my life. We named her Flicka, after the Mary O'Hara story. She carried me safely for hundreds of miles through the Cariboo bush. When it comes to understanding my lifelong love of horses, this honest, black pony is the one I must thank.

I know this now. I was born to ride, I was born to write.

As a girl, even when I was in trouble, the voice inside me was rising above, turning it into a story. The worse things got, the more worthwhile my suffering because it would make for a better read. But don't get me wrong. I did not grow up in a life of hardship. My days were filled with all the senses of a budding, lifelong love affair with horses. Like so many of you, they were somehow a part of who I was.

First, though, a word of warning. This is not a manual on horsemanship, philosophy or the state of the world.

Forty-five years of journaling, along with the best of the Keystone blogs, has been boiled down into one year in the saddle. Just one year, made up of many, in the life of a woman who eats too much, rarely darkens the church or gym door, sweeps her crumbs under the rug, lies about flossing and beds down with any one of her husband, cat or dog. She collects old clocks and horses, working well and otherwise.

These photographs and stories reflect a life spent among horses. And, like life, they jump around a bit.

Since age eight, I have ridden and observed during the day, then at night, I've written it all down. The pictures have been generously shared by friends ... or pulled from the far reaches of my sock drawer ... or the boxes under the stairs ... or even the door of the fridge. I hope they sit well with you.

I urge you to make this book your own! Mark it up, fold back the important corners, add your own doodles and notes. Let *Horse Woman* become a journal of your own time in the saddle. If you have questions or are ripe for a debate, I invite you to become a Keystoner — a Keystone Equine Facebook follower — and send me a message there. Join in on the comments and discussion that are a hallmark of our online group. Your voice matters and you will be heard.

WINTER
Hope

One of the comforts after many years in the saddle is that the seasons come around, seemingly without change. This lends a stability to how we handle the highs and lows of horsemanship but the sameness can have its drawbacks.

Those of us who live in the northern reaches find this time of year to be slim pickings. The days are filled with long, slow hours of darkness. We are not riding. Depression comes a-creeping. Our time with our horses feels like stolen moments, fiddling with stiff straps and frozen fingers, paying bills, cleaning stalls, mending blankets and throwing hay.

I am no different. Each year, it seems harder to get back into shape, to keep my chin up when the clock is ticking, or when it's been weeks since I've ridden. Instead of focusing on the lack in my winter existence, I have learned to love the glimmers of hope ... the dreams I allow myself for the summer to come ... the making of plans ... the exercises I can do with my horse and with my own body, to help transition into spring.

So, dig in. Read, enjoy, think of the future but don't be in too much of a rush. The winter months are all about self-care, rebuilding the relationship we have with our horses, seeing to all the little details that get lost in warm weather's grind. Stay cozy, take the time to read and absorb this wisdom ... and while you're at it, put on a good pot of soup.

GREAT EXPECTATIONS

Here's to another year.

While my thoughts keep straying back to green grass like so many errant sheep, I see Mike's knocked together a pristine stone boat for the new pony, Tom Jones. This replaces my old sled, a battered relic of many misadventures — planned for and otherwise — until its demise one sad day when I'd unhitched behind the bale truck. Mike went to feed cows and promptly backed over it, squashing it flat.

And so, the new year brings opportunities to get young ponies driving and old trucks and trailers overhauled. My workbench is piled with repairs and projects that have waited patiently for the passing of Christmas.

I'm signed up for another round of lessons, ever the eternal student, and can hardly wait to start. I've a good horse here, a rare opportunity for me to learn on one far more advanced than my usual thirty-day wonders. This is the best way to refine my feel and tune my technique. If we ride mainly colts and green horses, it's easy to lose sight of where we want them to end up. While Henry graces my life, he will remind me.

Lately, I've felt a huge need to de-clutter my life, to travel light. Negative thought patterns, uncomfortable clothing, junk drawers brimful ... all are getting the ol' heave-ho. In their place, I yearn for quiet space in which to breathe, to really bask in the glow of that which brings comfort. For me, it's time to stop gathering, yearning, wanting, collecting. It's time to know that I have enough. It's time to feel and experience and do ...

It's time to ride.

His name was Ali. Nothing in his nine years of living had prepared him for an ordinary day in real life. A bay Arabian gelding with haunted eyes and four white feet, Ali and I crossed paths only because my father was friends with his owner. The day Ali reared over backwards, crushing that man's daughter, my father offered to take him away. He became my new horse.

I don't remember much about getting Ali on our trailer, or anything about the haul home. What stayed with me was this: here was a horse I must not make mistakes on. I don't think he'd been abused as such. God had just made him a misfit in his own life. Ali would try to be friendly but he was repulsed by my hand. He would sweat if spoken to and my covetous gaze made his skin crawl.

I learned the meaning of "riding madly off in all directions". In his efforts to please me, Ali would rev his jets and every move I made was wrong. I'd settle in the saddle and he'd say, "Do I go now?" I'd tell him to wait. "Do I go now?" and I'd tell him to wait. Two or three false starts and we'd start plunging backwards, "If not that way, then this?!" Like the fishtailing of a car before its inevitable crash, Ali's emotions were caught in a momentous grip. I remember the foam from his bit running down my face, along with my miserable tears.

At the time, I was in a lesson program with a brilliant teacher. She observed my new horse with a sigh. It was then that Ali began his new life. Unable to handle so much as an exasperated thought from me, Ali responded to my carrying a paperback book whenever I rode him. He'd threaten to fly off the rails and I'd sit, quietly trying to read, until he'd calm down enough to go on. Because even our spoken words of praise felt like demands to him, we'd offer a piece of carrot whenever he'd come close to doing right.

It's a humbling thing to train a horse for whom nothing is hoped. Thank God, there were others for me to ride. For close to two years, Ali walked and stretched and walked some more. One day, Ali said he was ready to try a trot. When that seemed safe enough, he suggested a canter. Just a small, ordinary thing but I was riding through tears of joy.

They say there is a job for every horse. Ali and I had learned much but if I was to continue as an aspiring young rider, it would have eaten him alive. By the time he was schooling like a plain old uncomplicated horse, we knew it was time to find him his soft place.

Serendipity played a part when we learned of the autistic child in a horse-loving family, a boy in need of a sweet and honest partner on whom to wander the trails. In turn, Ali found his undemanding pilot, one who ignored the relentless pressures of time and competitive goals. It was a perfect fit. Even now, I can't help but think of my little bay teacher with a smile.

I've long struggled with my weight. No amount of schooling the horses and ponies, of getting them to a place where they can proudly represent me, could change the fact that I was getting too big to ride some of them — and too big to ride any of them really well.

I figured that just one small change — finding the kind of food I felt worthy of — could have a huge impact. Like so many of you, my life is an intricate knot of caring for family, personal growth and making a living; each little thing we do for ourselves will have benefits somewhere else. Or so it has been for me.

So far, I've said goodbye to around twenty pounds, just being careful, just being aware, admitting when my feelings are hurt or I'm lonely, inviting myself to take a walk instead of a cookie. A big part of this journey has been in learning to listen to my body and to stop stuffing with things that are my own personal poison.

I know I'm not alone. When we are larger than we want to be, we somehow become invisible. Looking at my wonderful horses, many of whom have changed their lives to become what I dream for them, is my incentive. If this is something you've been thinking about, just know that you can do it. It doesn't need to be fast, or expensive, or gimmicky, or within a time frame. It is simply a matter of loving oneself enough to enhance life.

Mindful little choices. One day, then another day, and then the next ...

Journaling. Valuable riding tool, or the making of a keepsake?

From the childhood Christmas when my mother gave me that first lovely, blank notebook, I've kept riding journals in which I've also sketched and written quotations, added news clippings and lessons I've learned.

The earliest of these journals are now forty-five years old and include everything from the big Pony Show at age eight, to the four years as a student with my German dressage teacher. I see reams of both useful information and teenage angst in those books.

To this day, even though I am taking lessons in a different discipline, I still come home, put the kettle on and think back to the golden message in the day's teaching. How did my teacher explain away the stiffness on my horse's left side? Or the struggle for those flying changes? I want to remember all these moments of difficulty, which are especially valuable, along with the inevitable breakthroughs.

In my daily riding, there is always at least one golden moment that deserves to be kept safe.

I want to talk about my special mental health geraniums. They have come with me through thick and thin, saved from a throwaway pile at the local greenhouse and the flower pots at my daughter's wedding.

Cut back, repotted and fertilized each autumn, they live here so that when I walk up the snowy path to the back door — arms aching with bags of groceries, pushing my way over power cords and shovels and boots kicked all asunder — there will be a long shelf of greenery and bright red flowers sending their blessings through the back porch's frosted glass.

When I fling open the door and call, "Hello, house!" there is the smell of a garden growing. See what I mean? I'm feeling better already.

Vince Lombardi, the quotable football coach, once said, "Practice doesn't make perfect; perfect practice makes perfect". It's a commendable notion but it's also a really unhealthy mindset, when it comes to training horses.

If we don't adhere to the 'one percent rule' of daily improvement, we run into dangerous territory. We won't practice unless we can do it perfectly or worse, we'll keep after the poor horse until he does.

So much of riding is based on learning feel and technique, plus building the appropriate muscle. For the horses to carry out our demands — all with a definite language barrier — it's a wonder they even try.

Perhaps a gentler and wiser approach to riding would be to 'practice being a little bit better, most of the time'? I know, it's not catchy as quotes go — but it's something to aspire to.

To be fair, broke means something different to each of us. To me, it's a calm and willing horse who will absolutely try his heart out; he'll neck rein and know the meaning of the word "whoa". In my world, broke also means a horse that can handle a cow or a trail ride and give me a good time at an open show.

In real speak, fifty percent of his saddle time will be climbing hills and hard riding; the other fifty percent is schooling in the arena, working on softening into the bridle, loping a pretty circle and achieving some semblance of speed control. I'm looking for the horse that has worked with the wind in his ears as much as he's darkened an arena door.

If you have an arena horse that can't work in the open, you are utilizing just fifty percent of your horse. It doesn't matter if he's into dressage or barrels. If he could learn to loose rein it and do an honest day's work in the great outdoors, his mind and body would thank you.

Conversely, if you mainly check cows or ride the trails, it's time to pimp your ride! Use that undeveloped fifty percent to teach your horse that all three gears have low, medium and high settings — and to maintain one of these until asked otherwise. Teach him about seeking a soft feel and about straight lines, circles and curves; teach him to understand your increasingly subtle aids. I repeat, his mind and body will thank you.

Too many of us are riding the wrong horse. We feel honour bound to keep trying because of money invested or the animal's prospects as a performance horse. What we don't consider is that to reach this potential, our horse or pony needs to be with someone who makes all things possible. If we are worried or fearful, he will be worried and fearful — and we will always hold one another back.

If your spirit does not soar when you sit in the saddle, I'm going so far as to say you're overmounted. The culture might tell you to 'cowboy up' but I believe that making yourself ride the wrong horse is nothing short of self-torture. If this sounds familiar, please give yourself the gift of saying you've had enough.

A healthy training program will have a method, with rules and expectations. It will also honour and respect the inherent uniqueness of each individual who passes through. This means that every horse or pony we school should pretty much go to a pattern. Whether we were to climb on one or the other, each would go to a standard and have the same buttons and switches installed. But it also means that even though there is a sameness to their training, we have not tried to make them the same.

One will always go slower, one will be more quick-legged; one will be light and round while the other might prefer a firmer contact, or more leg, or take more time to process the aids. This is good because it tells us we are still listening to the horses, all the while we are bending them to our will. Trust me, most of our horses would far prefer to stay home and eat. But when it is time to do our bidding, they will be reasonably happy because we have given them a task.

Then, we'll sit back and without ugly micro-managing, allow them to just get it done.

When a parent tells us a child no longer wants to ride their pony, or that "they're just not that into it", it's a red flag of warning. Kids, whether yours, mine, or the whole neighbourhood's, will ride and groom the hair off a good pony, because they're having that much fun.

If this is a phrase you've been hearing, either from your own child about his current ride, or from sellers explaining why their pony is for sale, take heed. A solid pony will instill such a love of horsemanship, you'll have to protect him to give him a moment's peace.

Among the attributes for a good first pony, one we hold especially dear is our "Rule of Twenty". It's a formula so solid that whenever we're pairing junior riders and performance ponies, we want their ages to total at least twenty years.

When you go for a test ride, you are on trial as much as the horse. The seller will note how comfortably correct you are in handling, haltering, tying, grooming, picking feet, saddling, bridling … and these things will tell him as much about your ability as your equitation will when you climb aboard.

The more you speak of your knowledge, the less you will appear to know and yes, it's within the seller's right at any time to refuse you the ridden trial. After all, he or she wants to keep you alive. Do not argue, do not get huffy. The seller knows his horse better than you do and your wounded pride is preferable to a broken neck. Remember that even if you love the horse, you are not necessarily his best match.

While trial riding, wear safe and appropriate clothing, be punctual, happily sign the waiver when asked, don't tire the horse out or take up the seller's day. If you don't like the horse when you ride him, quietly dismount, hand the seller the reins and say he's not what you need but be polite and thank the seller for his time.

Please, don't blame the animal's Western or English schooling, his lack of spirit, the make of the saddle or the style of the reins. Should you do so, you are underlining the fact that more mileage is needed and that you would be better served with a dedicated teacher and a regular riding program, rather than a new horse.

If you're already in lessons, make sure you are shopping with the blessing of your teacher. Few buyers seem to think this through. It's best to bring your coach along on the trial. Be businesslike, be prepared to pay this person for their time and expertise. It will be money well spent and ultimately the kindest thing for your new equine friend. Out of decency and respect for the horse, please limit the number of people you bring along to climb aboard for 'a little go'. It is enough to see the seller ride the horse, then the teacher, then the student.

Lastly, it is expected that you call if you are lost, or are otherwise going to be late, or if you have simply changed your mind. It alarms me that good manners have become so very rare.

I did something stupid yesterday. Whenever we do and somehow don't get hurt, we can call ourselves lucky. The wind was blowing cold off the Rockies and I decided that my new horse, Pilot, could use a warmer blanket. He's a good guy and stands quietly while I fuss with his straps, so I didn't bother haltering him. Worse, I didn't bother taking a look to see where we were in relation to the other horses.

While I was reaching underneath, one of the others went after him. I was knocked off my feet and when the moment had passed, Pilot was standing on my hand. Thanking my good fortune that the afternoon sun had melted the frozen ground, I was lucky to get away with just a bruising. It was a reminder that if you can't see the eye of the boss hoss in a loose group of horses, you're taking chances. Why? Because he can't see you.

I know better. Still, it might be a vanishing bit of knowledge, just being aware of how to navigate a loose herd of horses. A world unto its own, there is social climbing, the pecking order, greed, lust and jealousy, enough to rival the steamiest of soap operas. At the best of times, a group of horses is a shifting mass of energy, petty squabbles and hurts that might have happened long before we show up at the corral ... and they're not always mindful of who's in the way when it's time to even the score.

We can easily be kicked or run over when standing in a milling group, as jealousy between loose horses, grudges, mares in heat and newcomers all play a part in their socialization. None of these scenarios takes into consideration whether individuals within the herd actually respect our personal space or not. Sometimes, we just get hidden or are in the wrong spot.

I'm super cautious going out to a herd with a pail of grain. I prefer my horses to stand quietly while I walk up, sans treats, to catch them with halters, before leading them out. When I was a kid, the old-timers used to have their horses whip broke, so that when you flicked a lead rope in their direction, the whole herd would stop and head up to face you.

Turning out is another area to use caution. Always let the lower horse in the pecking order go, first. He can be gone and away before you let loose the thug.

Remember, if you can't see the dominant horse's eye when you're haltering or leading another one, you're not safe. Why? Because he can't see you.

Well, heck. I've been expecting my horse to be better than I am and she's telling me that's not her job.

She's been struggling with walk-to-lope transitions. When I ask for third gear, she will either: a) ignore me b) swing her hips in c) open her mouth d) ask for more rein or e) all of the above. My answer to this has been to paste a smile on my face and be grateful for the time and place she eventually offers it up.

This past week, I've finally decided to get real. This is a problem and needs looking into. Hiding stuff is another of my specialties, like sweeping toast crumbs under the refrigerator. So, I went back and: a) asked myself when the problem arose b) used the smooth ring snaffle and two hands c) took off my spurs d) reinstalled the meaning of my legs by supporting them with a dressage whip, before e) reinstalling the meaning of my hands via the soft feel.

Then, perhaps ten minutes later, the mare offered up one beautiful, round, quiet, happy transition after another. Everything else about riding her got better, too. Seems I've been busy sweeping too many 'crumbs' out of sight. The moral of this story? Don't expect your horse to be better than you are. That's not her job.

Rebuilding an old saddle.

My body is tired but my mind says I haven't much to show for my effort, to keep on keeping on. Of course, my hand slips; I make a costly mistake. Disgusted, disheartened, I head outside to find solace. The east wind is colder than I'd thought, life feels hard and I'm tired plumb through to my bones.

Trudge, trudge, trudge, down a draw and I come upon the horses. They're friendly but frankly, not all that interested in my woes. I rub a few foreheads and, with a new take on life and the wind behind me, head happily back to the house. Such is their gift to me.

Another birthday.

Gotta say, there was a time I didn't think I'd see many more of them, so that's changed how I feel about growing older. I am at the age where we can wonder what we've done with our lives, however. We see other people who have achieved so much. It's easy to feel that we're somehow lacking.

I have moments of this, too. Every year, a new round of vows to: take better care of myself; save more money; go on that trip; repair friendships; finish painting the house; improve the garden; learn to dance or sing or write a book or win a buckle or make good bread or... You know?

It did occur to me — while eating birthday cheesecake for breakfast, in bed — that if I was given the chance to go back to being younger, would it be all that I remember? Would having shiny brown hair and straighter, whiter teeth be compensation for self-doubt and inexperience? Would years of mixed up living really be preferable to my wonky hip and bigger jeans? No, I doubt that they would.

Instead, let's all vow to be a bit wiser, kinder and more aware of what's going on around us, with each and every year. Let's look after ourselves so that we may age with as much grace as possible. Let's strive to be whole enough, well enough, involved enough, to somehow serve.

There. I've blown out my little candle and made my wish.

The Name Game: do you change a horse's pet name when he comes to you, or do you stay the course? This is on my mind right now as I await the arrival of this latest in a long line of individuals to grace my life. Do I have any right, beyond this shiny new transfer of ownership, to change the story of who this fellow is? A lovely horse, who he is has very little bearing on what the dictionary says his name means, "Gadget: a thing to make a job easier but not an essential tool to keep." Nope, I'm not feelin' it.

Cowboy wisdom tells us it's plumb bad luck to change a horse's name. That, I think, is not always true. The pony that comes with the name, Killer, surely deserves something else. The others, like Henry — sailing through life with grace and a sense of humour, always bathed in love and knowledge — have no reason for an alias. They are who they are.

I'm learning, however, that horses with stories like Henry's are in the minority. Besides, one can know only so many Magics and Annies and Ciscos in this life.

Do horses know their pet names? Heck, do they even care? Of course, they do. But if their names cause us to speak of them differently, to feel a remembered fear or shame, I harbour no regrets at re-labelling. Thus, Killer becomes Winchester, Babe becomes Brown Betty, Pony becomes Tom Jones... and judging by their stories, they've seized all the possibilities that come with positive change. My friends will never be called Spook, or Diablo, or Fury, simply because I think we all rise to whatever is hoped of us, however high or low the bar is set.

I'm thinking all this, as I wait by the highway, searching the darkness for oncoming lights.

If you're like me, you learn best from your mistakes. The speeding ticket on the way home, the pasture gate left open because there's nary a horse in sight, the seafood at the dodgy all-you-can-eat buffet... Sigh. So why is it so hard to allow others, especially those we love, to make them?

Do we want to spare them the distress of learning or do we just want to be in control at all times? This hard question is particularly apt in our riding. Whenever we allow the horse to deviate — within the parameters of safety — we can help him. This is how he learns and how we lend support.

Examples of this process might be the horse that struggles with self-carriage or speed control; the horse that has a hard time passing the out gate at the arena; the horse that is learning to watch a cow. Good news is, there is no end of opportunity to master this in our horsemanship.

Too often, we'll ride as though we're being judged. This mindset makes us cautious, always playing it safe by babysitting the horse. We nag, he tunes us out, ad infinitum. He does not progress, we stay stuck ... and then, we wonder why?

Ever have a friend who only calls if she needs something? Me, too — and it doesn't take long before I grow wary. So often, especially if our animals live away, we only see them when we want to work them. Soon, they're not quite over the moon when we show up.

As often as I can, I drop in on my horses just to chill out, to stand visiting, keeping my hands to myself and asking how their day goes? The old-timers might get scratched in favourite places — but the youngsters are treated with more restraint. I don't want them getting too off-hand or demanding of my space.

For that reason, I don't go out to the herd with treats. I count legs and eyeballs, straighten a few forelocks, then leave. With the aloof ones, it's enough just getting them to stand and soak up my saying they're smart and handsome, without them moving off. Stabled horses can be chatted up as we pick through their bedding, freshen water pails and feel if they're too warm. Take the tired or inward fellow out for a grazing walk; it will do you both a world of good.

Simply put, visits like these are deposits into the 'good feelings' account. When we start showing and training, the withdrawals will sure add up.

If there was one use for my written thoughts, it would be to bring all of us here from our separate disciplines. Our worlds where tempo and engagement matters, where the turnaround does, the eye for a distance as opposed to watching a cow, the lead change, the pace along the marathon, that one last hill to climb, the leaders, the wheelers, the strides, the lines, the rundown and stop, the final halt and salute.

What happens here is that for a while, we forget about our differences and we talk about this thing we all love.

One of the bits of horsemanship that irks me is the tendency towards a polarity of beliefs and methodologies. You know, "I follow this person, or this method, or this discipline … " when I rather suspect that the horse is a forgiving creature and will work for any one of us if we have conviction and follow through and quit jumping from ship to ship.

What I remember from my youth is the ordinary teachers who were just really good working horsemen; older men, most often, who had colts all the way to superstars in their barns, men who rode cutters and could school harness ponies and open jumpers. That type of horseman might be on the endangered list nowadays and I'm suggesting we're the worse for it.

These horsemen got this way from living and breathing horses. They predated a time where people went to the barn for an hour a week. So, they shoveled and doctored, fed and hot-walked, took lessons, taught lessons and rode all the difficult horses on their way to show ring glory. They knew the industry all the way from taking the books to the banker, to getting the chore tractor going in the cold. Many of them could repair a saddle, nail on a shoe and buck out a cold-backed horse, should the need arise.

The one fellow that most comes to mind for me, Bill Collins, was a man who put Canadian cutting on the map but also tended his show hunters. We rarely see the likes of these horsemen, any more.

Why should we care? I do, because it's a fact of life that we've fewer young barn rats just hanging around any more, taking in their horsemanship by osmosis, the way the old horsemen did as kids. We've fewer people listening in and observing, watching what other disciplines involve and seeing what those horses and riders do that makes their sports so good.

What we can do, however, is to open a conversation and get to know one another, maybe get inspired to step out and mix things up a bit, try something new and different. This openness, growing comfortable in each other's company, is something I believe in with all my heart. Thanks for being part of it.

On plans and regrets ...

This time of year, it's natural to look ahead and make dreams for the future; it's natural to look back and relive memories, both painful and good. I've long ago stopped making new year's resolutions. No matter what I called them, they were just another way to beat myself up.

This past year has seen friends achieve the victory of dreams, while others face unimaginable loss and sorrow. I am grateful to be plodding along the middle ground; giving thanks for year-round water in my pens today, along with a beautiful outdoor training ring, for both of which I've waited years. This summer saw the replacement of another mile or so of fence — no big deal to anyone but Mike and me — and these new posts and wires stretch along lines built between the 1920s and the second world war. It was time.

Best of all, we welcomed my son-in-law, another Lee, into our family.

New homes were found for four Keystone ponies and horses in the past months. Now, four more enthusiastic owners are riding for the brand. One mare is leased to further her education and there are new faces looking out over the corral. These always make me feel rich, somehow, as I contemplate fresh opportunities, raise my hopes and start to plan.

There are threads of sadness woven into this cloth of mine: friends who grow distant; clients I'm unable to please; horses and ponies that are not up to whatever life demands. The list is a short one, yet makes itself known in those hours before dawn.

My goals will stay small ones. To better enjoy the moments with which I'm blessed. To nurture and value those who adore me. To recognize when the animals in my care are giving their best. To go long, safe miles doing this thing I love. To pay my way, to help others, to try and be kind and wise and strong and good.

What I really want is for each of us to find some sort of peace in the here and now. For that alone, yes.

TOO COLD TO RIDE?

For those of us who ride and live in a certain geography, this time of year can be slim pickings. We want to get out there, we yearn to improve and yet sometimes, we just can't. It is time for the practice of gratitude. Oh, please don't groan. Get a pencil and paper and begin. Not feelin' it? OK, I'll go first ...

Sunday mornings with a cup of coffee and the company of a loyal dog. New winter tires. My online community of friends. Listening to the horses munching after I've struggled to do winter chores. My boots with new insoles. The plans I make for the summer. But for now, maybe just starting a pot of stew.

I'm especially grateful for the new year-round water that my mother had installed in our pens. Or my tack room, now clean. I've donated all the safe but unused tack and grooming tools to a local 4-H club. Before, it went to therapeutic riding. Needing inspiration, I've printed and framed a couple of last summer's pictures to put around the house. I go for walks. I know, it's darned cold but it feels good to get out there. There's beautiful hoar frost on the trees.

I sing. Even if just in the shower or around the house, singing brings happiness. I make friends with my favourite riding books again. There is relief in booking the trailer for its annual safety check. I'm grateful to be signing up for lessons. It doesn't even have to be riding, it can be anything. It's a gift to myself to learn something new.

There's a buzz that comes from taking an hour and going through our show clothes. What fits this year and what does not? What needs cleaning, or buttons sewn on, alterations or repair? What is getting 'tired out' or ready to go on its journey? Cold weather projects are: the boots that need polishing or a dye job to match my chaps; the hat that needs cleaning or shaping; the wool show pads that need a good brushing to again look like new.

When it's too cold to ride, I take a long, hard look at myself and vow to improve my turnout. I might look online for pictures of someone who I respect in my discipline. I'll compare what they have done to look right and where I might make changes. Being well turned out isn't about money. It's about a relentless attention to detail, the mark of someone who has a passion and respect for the horse.

When the kids were young, I would make sure their riding and show clothes fit for the coming year. If not, we had time to alter them, or shop for what we needed, second hand.

If I'm completely honest, I am sometimes grateful for the break from it all. Winter brings the chance to catch my breath, to stop doing and start appreciating again. In the summer, there is so much needing to be done, even beyond the horses. Lawns must be mowed, flowers kept watered, lessons to teach, shows to attend, feed put up, buildings and fences painted and repaired. I'm grateful that these things always herald the summer but I'm really grateful that they don't need my attention right now.

If I'm lucky, there's the special horse that allows me to go out dressed like the abominable snowman, climb the fence and slide on to his warm, fuzzy back. Why, as we age, do we forget the joy of riding bareback in the snow?

When it's too cold to ride, I try and get 'the other stuff' done. You know, the new blades for the clippers. The stitching fixed on my reins. The health records brought up to date, the registration papers printed and organized for the upcoming shows. Memberships bought. Prize lists applied for. The horses' teeth done, along with their vaccinations and any needed tests noted and scheduled before we hit the road.

When it's too cold to ride, I do the next best thing and work my horses from the ground. I haul once or twice a week to an arena with good footing but here at home, the ground is like cast iron, if not covered with drifts of snow. If it's not too slippery, I can bundle up, put the cavesson and lunge rein on the horses and still be a part of their lives. This constancy is key in keeping them going, if they're still somewhat green.

The older horses are turned away for the winter, to run in a herd and play stallion games. They come back in the spring, fresh and full of fun.

The ones kept in will work on voice commands, gymnasticizing and stretching in walk and trot (even canter, if not too icy), always in both directions. For fun, I'll teach them how to sidle up to the mounting block and stand. Some days are scheduled for tender, loving care and little else. They will melt in one spot while I go over them with a favourite brush, tidying them up, just putting my hands on in something other than my usual taking away.

This is the time of year to book sessions, for both ourselves and our horses, with the chiropractor and for massage. Whether we have longstanding stiffness from past injuries or whether we grow stiff from standing clenched in the cold, on icy ground, these things do wonders for keeping us agile and ready to go to work in the spring.

When it's too cold to ride, I like to teach the new horses and ponies to put their own halters on. I put my right arm over their polls and wait patiently, without being aware of the pressures of time and performance, teaching them to lower their heads. By holding the halters open below their noses, it's not too long before they are reaching down with their muzzles and helping. Strangely, this has made all of them easier to catch. Without grain or treats, they are happy to help and to show their new skills. Best of all, it starts each session off with submission, praise and trust.

These are also the days that I will work on loading into the trailer. When we have all the time in the world, loading takes minutes. When we have mere minutes, loading a horse can take all the time in the world. When his response becomes quiet and without question, then we're getting somewhere. Now we can haul.

I spend a lot of time with my young, green or herdbound horses, hauling alone on short trips. We'll go to the grocery store or to get the mail, then home again. They learn that no matter where we go, we'll come back. It's a valuable lesson. This way, no horse or pony is hauling for his first time to the show or an emergency trip to the vet.

If we're housebound and itching to do something, we can stir up a bunch of horse cookies to take to the barn. There are easy recipes online and even if we don't make a practice of feeding our horses by hand (and I don't usually, but that's a discussion for another time), a few homemade cookies slipped in with the supper ration will be appreciated. We all like to show — and be shown — unconditional love.

When winter feels long 'n' hard and I need my horse fix, I'll bring what I love inside. I knew that when I grew up, if ever I did, that my home would be a place where my dogs and all my horse things were welcome. I'll dust off and decorate the mantelpiece with special ribbons and trophies, some beloved pictures. In the corner of the dining room, I'll set up my favourite sidesaddle. While conditioning the leather, I smile and remember fabulous rides and long-ago summers.

It helps me remember that my life, even in darkest winter, is good.

Too cold to ride? Just get outside.

When the temps drop, it's important to keep a close eye on the horses and ponies that are turned out. Really cold weather has them needing as much water as they do in summer's heat — and don't believe the old myth that they can go eat snow. The colic threat ramps up in winter and old-timers, especially, need a close watch whenever it's icy underfoot. Their fear of falling will actually trump their need to eat and drink.

We had a lot of snow and wind damage in the yard this year and I've been kept busy, dragging tree branches over to the pit. As I was doing this, I spied our newest pony standing nearby. Perfect.

Haltering the gelding, I let him tag along at the end of the lead rope and went back to work. Billy educated me in mere seconds about what made him tick. When pressured — that is, asked to leave the herd or do anything he didn't sign up for — he had a meltdown. Good to know. We kept slogging, despite his protestations and soon, he was helping out like a real hand. Together, we had a productive day.

So much behavioural stuff is helped by chugging along, doing our yard work, raking, picking pens, wheeling the manure cart ahead of the pony. We sort of forget he's there; he sort of forgets to fight us. Call it ridiculous, but this harmless desensitizing is a real boon when we start working these guys in harness.

Training to handle pressure comes wherever, whenever. Don't let the teachable moments pass you by.

A little skill to work on during the off season is training your horse to relieve himself at your prompting.

Race horse trainers — and mothers of toddlers in one-piece snow suits — have long known that the day is greatly enhanced if bladders are empty. The practical applications for your average horse or pony are: increased comfort during long hauls; keeping your trailer floor dry; less everyday stall cleaning and bedding waste; proof that they are or are not drinking enough; stress-free gathering of urine samples for drug testing or health care; less time in the wash racks and increased performance in competition.

Besides, it's a great way to dazzle your friends.

Remember, our horses are creatures of habit. If you're watchful, you'll see that they relieve themselves in pretty much the same place at the same time, day in, day out. Start giving them a signal — I like to whistle — whenever this happens and praise them when they're done. While this has zero to do with you at first, it sets them up for success.

In a few days, you can halter one and take him over to where he usually stales, start whistling and Bob's yer uncle. Allow the horse to face into the wind if you're outdoors and just start making it a mindful business. Soon enough, you'll be able to back your horse off the trailer on cross country hauls and set him up for the pause that refreshes.

So often when we're showing a horse that isn't quite on his game, a horse that is restive or just doesn't want to extend or hold his pace, it's because he'd like to relieve himself and doesn't quite know how to go about it during the hurly burly of competition.

Staling on command gives you one more tool in your tool box. I've had my own horses do this for close to forty years and it's worth the wee effort. Sorry, I couldn't resist.

Believe it or not, the way our horse or pony loads is indicative of our mutual respect. There is more than one way to load successfully; if your horse gets on calmly, quietly, every single time out, then you're doing it right. The following method has worked well for us, whether we're loading horses, ponies or cattle.

We start by getting some respect for our personal space by round-penning the pony. When asked, we want her to calmly and obediently move forward, backward and change direction, without a halter or rope. It's a small step to clip on a long shank and ask for the same manoeuvres — and if she's learned her ground work well, she won't step on us or kick at us when we send her forward. It's an easy thing to see if she's moving off us by stepping over a horse blanket on the ground …

Once we can send our pony over plywood or mud puddles, it's an easy step to send her into the waiting trailer. No whips, no treats, just trust. If she says no, then we calmly step back from the trailer and send her back to work around us, until she's puffing and ready to renegotiate. As long as she faces the trailer, she doesn't get put to work.

A note here about 'helpers' … if they want to sit and watch, that's fine. But they must promise not to talk to you, do any urging or clucking, pressuring you or the horse mentally or physically. Our goal is a horse or pony that loads without outside assistance, each and every time.

Here's the biggest mistake people make when a green horse trusts them enough to load: they slam the door shut. Don't. Wait and ask the pony to back out calmly. If she rushes back, then put her to work again behind the trailer before asking her to reload. The door isn't ready to be closed until the pony is calmly, happily standing in the safety of the trailer. You should have to tell her when it's time to step off.

I should add here that we seldom tie in the trailer. We have our personal reasons based on where we haul, the type of trailer we use and often, it just feels safer for us, too. However, we teach our horses to haul both ways. If she wants to turn around in the slant haul, she gets tied. If she's the aggressor while hauling with other horses, she gets tied. If she's a guest on someone else's trailer, she gets tied.

Our goal is to make a pony that travels straight without turning around, one that can be trusted to haul, holding her head wherever it's comfortable. This isn't always doable due to certain circumstances and if we don't trust them, they get tied. Usually, the lead rope is simply passed over the top of the divider to keep it easy to reach and out from underfoot. It can as easily be laid across the horse's back.

When we unload, we usually back out, unless it is too slippery to do this safely. Why? There's nothing worse than having a horse turn on you and rush the door. Besides, backing up is an ongoing lesson in respect that works wonders. It builds trust and is just good horsemanship to ask for a step and wait … and ask for a step and wait …

Finally, standing half-way in and stepping forward or backward according to your whim is excellent training. After a long haul or a big day showing, this position is wonderful for stretching the lumbar. Our experienced travellers always pause for a stretch and a moan as they unload.

If you remember to make it a pleasant experience to be in the trailer — and this includes how you handle your rig on the road — your horse or pony will learn to relax and enjoy the trip.

Suitability. It's a broad word that means more than not pairing the six-foot tall working cowboy with the Shetland pony. While I would question how many horses truly share our dreams and aspirations (mine, I know for a fact, would rather eat, sleep and lounge around), the travesty of putting high hopes onto the backs of horses who are unable to carry them off, is all too common.

As my life has gone through its dips and turns, certainly my goals have as well. It's an evolution of sorts and that's okay. I no longer feel a person is wasting a talented horse if they choose only to wander mountain trails. If the horse safely enjoys these sojourns, then they're suited. It really doesn't matter that he's worth as much as a nice car. If they're both happy, it's cool.

What does matter, however, is when I project what I want and need onto an animal that can't do it without self-destructing. Whether mentally or physically, such use of him is morphing uncomfortably into abuse.

For a long time, I wanted to compete at a higher level in combined driving. I really liked driving my ponies but I wanted something bigger, stronger, with more jam. Eventually, I bought myself a young Welsh Cob. Eddie was unstarted, a blank slate, just the most spectacular guy imaginable. Representing centuries of animals bred to drive and move at a huge trot, he and I would be brilliant. Of this, I was absolutely certain.

Well, of course, he hated driving. We got him going but he loathed everything about it. I was finally forced to admit that my dream was destroying his confidence. Ouch. Eddie wanted to serve — but he wanted to serve under saddle. It didn't matter what, he'd just rather do anything than go driving with me.

In the end, I made the decision to sell him and while this was hard, it was exciting to see him excel in his new sport, in new hands. Which leads me to believe: If you love 'em, you'll either change sports to suit 'em, or you'll send 'em down the road.

We have somehow indoctrinated ourselves into believing that selling our horses is cruel and irresponsible, that they'll suffer in other hands or they'll be packed to the cannery at Fort Macleod. That's possible but it's not probable — and it's self-serving thinking, if we're in a relationship with a horse that can't cope with our demands. This might mean changing our dreams of western pleasure glory for ones of competitive trail, or letting our cow-bred horse go off to the hunter ring, or retiring from campaigning when a beloved horse can no longer take the long hauls.

Does it put the onus on us to investigate other avenues in our horsemanship? Yes. Will it be hard learning something new? Yes. Will we cry and gnash our teeth if they need to go on without us? Perhaps.

Bottom line, I am not urging anyone to dump their horse like a jug of bad milk. No, the challenge is in seeing how open we are to adjusting our hopes and dreams to matching the horses we profess to care for. If they are not suitable, we can change expectations, we can change horses. Or we can continue forcing them to do that of which they are physically or mentally incapable. Always, the choice is our own.

"Ours is not to question why, ours is but to do and die ..." For soldiers or horses, Alfred, Lord Tennyson said it best.

During a recent riding lesson, clients and I were discussing saddle fit and how to go about evaluating this while the saddle was on the horse. "First, check the fit without the blanket," I said, "nudge the saddle back to just behind the shoulder, then feel with your hand held flat, palm up, between the bar of the tree and the horse ..."

That's when I heard an exclamation from the other side. "There's a nail sticking out of the saddle!" A common nail had worked its way out from underneath the saddle, pressing sharply into the horse. A hammer was fetched, the nail pulled and another lesson learned. This would've been a nail that was put in when the high-end custom saddle was built. It should've been pulled but was somehow forgotten. Trust me, we gave heartfelt thanks and apologies to the saintly beasts that had carried the rig.

An unfortunate occurrence, I've found nails that have worked their way out of our own saddles, too. All I know to prevent this is to be faithful in checking one's equipment — with eyes and fingertips — in strong light.

Stallion games, the endless biting matches that go on and on.

These games are an important part of living within the herd and horses that understand such contests are showing us that they are joyful, as well as socialized. They are neither bullying, nor avoiding contact.

These games of one-up-man-ship interest me, as they are found almost exclusively within a group of geldings. Mares, for the most part, have better things to do with their day, than chew on each other's knee caps.

When we stop what we are doing, really pause and look, we are reminded that there is more to this gig than cleaning stalls, paying for feed and finding those lead changes. We laugh and cheer for the underdog. Our horses realize that they bring more to our relationships than just those heavy things mentioned above.

When we start to pay attention, we see that our horses get so much pleasure from entertaining us. I've noticed that when a round of stallion games is about to begin, the boys manage to stage them right in front of the big window in the house.

Stabled horses sometimes do not understand the social strata within a herd and they have to be taught. Oh, the squeals, the heels and chunks of flying hair. But this one thing is very good for their mental and physical health.

Best of all, our horses train better, eat better, and have fewer overall complications when they are allowed to play just as hard as they work.

After over thirty years of marriage, romance is wherever you can find it. I came across Mike today, doing a beautiful job of steaming and reshaping my old hat. When I gushed my thanks, he looked deep into my eyes and said, "I don't like you looking dorky."

Be still, my heart. What more could a girl ever want?

I asked a friend recently if she'd missed riding her horse with all the cold weather. She thought about it for a moment, then said, "Honestly? No." She then proceeded to tell me why.

Her life has been very stressful with business, health and family issues, so when she starts feeling pressured, riding is the first thing to go. Instead of beating herself up, she does her chores and sweeps the aisle, listening to the sounds of contented horses stamping, snorting, munching. She gives thanks.

She catches one horse and gives her a beauty makeover, or just a mindful, meaningful grooming session. She feels appreciated.

She takes her buddy to the pen and works on lungeing exercises, asking her to go forward in a long, swingy rhythm — or she puts long reins on and they head out for a driving walk. She gets some exercise and fresh air.

She cleans her equipment and checks the soundness of reins, billets and latigos for the coming year. She looks after her safety.

She visualizes what it will be like when she can get riding again and thinks about doable goals and expectations. She allows herself to hope and dream.

Horsemanship comes to any one of us, however we invite it in. Not being able to ride isn't the end of the world.

Despite wanting it to be otherwise, we learn the most from the things that don't work out. Giving up on the problem horse that can't — or doesn't want to — get better is one of them.

We'll play all the 'what ifs' over and over in our minds, especially those times we can't sleep. We'll see the empty corral that used to have the familiar face hanging over the gate and rather than feeling free, we'll feel as though we're packing around a bad secret.

Once we decide to stop going 'round and 'round, never quite forgiving ourselves for quitting, it can sometimes take a while to build the sheer energy needed to go on to the next project. A new start should fill us with excitement but it can take a surprising amount of time when hope and all the try that's deep inside us, is finally dead.

I know this feeling. Despite having gone through it many times, it still takes a while to tromp my way through all the steps and admittedly, that often includes beating myself up. Just know that there's no expiry date on grief and disappointment. All I can promise is that if this is you, you are not alone and yes, this compassion and connection to our horses sometimes takes us to a very dark place. Hold on, keep your eyes up and eventually, you'll ride into the light.

I'm often asked if there's a correct way to put on and take off a horse blanket? Yes, there is. It's a good question and one that could be pondered by more people who've owned horses long enough to know this.

First off, after a close call recently, I'll start by saying we'd best halter the horse for both putting on and taking off those blankets. Live and learn. Many of us get lazy and leave the chest straps fastened; we blanket by pulling the whole thing over the horse's head. Horses can be made to accept this, absolutely, but it's not the best or safest method.

I prefer to blanket by loosely gathering the blanket over the arm closest to the horse's head, running the forearm straight along the centre seam where the horse's spine goes. It's an easy thing to swing this in one movement onto the withers of the horse. We'll fasten the top and bottom neck straps, then slide the blanket back into position when this is done.

Never pull the blanket ahead on a horse, as pulling against the hair causes discomfort and will surely make them cranky. Then we'll do the front surcingle, then the back surcingle. If the blanket has leg straps, I'll often not cross these to reduce the backwards pull on the shoulders, just a personal thing. The belly surcingles must be adjusted to the place where we can put our balled-up fist between them and the horse's belly, no looser.

Check that the surcingles are not twisted. Rubber rings for sheep castration can be had from the local feed store. These can be slipped over buckles that tend to come unfastened. If you don't have these rubber rings, fasten the first strap, then run the second strap between the doubled loop of the first. If one comes undone, it will be held off the ground without getting stepped on and ripped off.

Then, and only then, will we do up the leg straps. These will rub on a horse if they're not linked as a chain, so do the near side strap, go 'round to the off side and run this strap through the near side one before fastening. This link holds each strap off the delicate skin of the inside hind legs. This method is preferable to crossing the straps from one side to the other. Why? Because we can clip each strap to the same side we are standing on.

Unblanketing is pretty much the reversal of the above. I'm usually careful to re-clip the long elastic leg straps to the D rings when I pull blankets — this, after a long-ago wreck when they became tangled up and caught underneath a jumpy horse. It takes only a second to do this. Next, the surcingles under the belly, then the straps at the front.

Whenever we undo the front first, even if just for a few minutes to band or braid a horse, we open up a huge possibility for a wreck: the blanket slides back and the horse, particularly if he is young or nervous, panics. The blanket, still girthed up, does not fall away but drags along until kicked free.

Should a good horse panic? Of course not, but that's not always how horses think. Other than this, when we pull the blanket off, fold the front back over the loins and slide the whole thing off in the direction of the hair growth, for comfort's sake. The blanket is now folded correctly to go back on again.

Be careful when next touching or petting the horse — if his blanket is nylon, our next contact will be a shocking one. Grounding ourselves on a wooden fence or stall partition will help the zaps.

The failure to link the hind leg straps is the second biggest mistake we make while blanketing. The first big mistake is in failing to fasten from front to back and unfasten from back to front! Blanket statements? Perhaps, but they may well save a life.

Note: It was interesting to find that the above blanketing safety rule is followed only in certain parts of the world. Our fellow horsemen in Australia and New Zealand do the reverse. They fasten back to front. But fastening front to back was how I was trained. In light of the mesh and woollen coolers we northerners use having neck fastenings only, I must stand by how I was taught.

On the road again ...

When the ground gets hard and the wind blows cold, keep on truckin'. One of the best kept secrets for learning patience, manners and the ability to leave the herd is found in heading down the road. We take all our youngsters and any herdbound ponies for solo trailer rides ... to the grocery store, to pick up our mail, even to have coffee with friends.

The first few trips are hairy ones. The ponies lack confidence and the trailer is bouncing and banging while we're parked in front of the bank! By the third ride, however, they've figured it out. No matter where we've been, we always go home again. It's an important lesson and this method keeps everybody safe and able to think. By the way, leave the pony on the trailer until he's standing quietly, no matter how long it takes. Unloading during a tantrum will make a poor hauler who paws and frets for life.

Be it resolved that no horse or pony should have his first haul from home during an emergency trip to the vet.

The sun's shining, birds are singing, hair is flying everywhere. If you've left your beasts out in the back forty this winter, they mightn't be as keen as you to get back in the saddle again. Don't worry, there's a lot you can do to set the mood.

After long layoffs, we always bring the herd in, halter them, do their feet, saddle up and leave them tied up to 'soak' for an hour or two. A few days back in polite society, a bit of work in the round pen or on the lunge line and they're ready to talk. This lets us get a feel for the ones that remember the good ol' days — and the ones that might need a little more time in ground school. Set yourself up for success — and stay safe out there.

Still too cold to ride? Well, it's not too cold to make plans for the upcoming show season.

This year, vow to improve your turnout. Why is it some folks can show for years and still manage to look messy? Turnout has little to do with dollars; it has everything to do with details. Observe one of your heroes and compare. Be ruthless.

Here are my top ten ways to rise above the crowd: Feed correctly. Protect your horse's coat and tail. Groom him, the old-fashioned way, with care and effort.

Learn to band or braid perfectly, which will involve a lot of practice. If your buckles don't align on your bridle, if the headstall isn't neat, now is the time to have the saddler make it so. Clean your tack.

Clothes need to be classic, quality and well-fitted. Do something with your hair. Trim the ends off your spur straps, tuck up too-long stirrup leathers. If you're not competing in dressage, then ditch the dressage pad.

One more bonus tip for western gals. Please, no sparkles below the belt, be tasteful to the point of severity, shape your hats and yes, saddle pads and jackets need to match.

Picky and unrelenting? Yep. But turnout is one area where we can, almost all of us, improve.

SADDLE UP

Every Monday morning, long before daylight, I throw back the covers, dress quickly, knock back a slug of coffee, whistle up the dog and pull on my boots. We step out into the inky dark and go in search of the horses.

I realize that I am truly blessed to be among the few who welcome Mondays. It wasn't always thus. First, there were those awful weekday mornings while I was in school and then, it was my turn getting our own kids out the door. Begging them to 'please eat something so that the teachers couldn't say the McLean kids weren't fed!' I also drove other peoples' children to school, a job I did for eighteen years.

But enough of that. I'm excited for Mondays because once again, I've signed up for lessons. This marks my eighth winter, hauling in to an ag society arena about an hour's drive from here. While it's not at all convenient hunting one's pastured horses down in the January pre-dawn, nor making the 196 km (122 mile) round trip on winter roads, I love it.

Why? Well, these lessons get me through the dark months. I relish the camaraderie of this handful of riders that I've met weekly over the years. Our teacher is the main reason we all go, of course. I've yet to see another coach so able to take a bewildering array of riders and horses, keeping all improving week to week, keeping all on task for the hour or so we meet, keeping all keen for more and somehow, staying sane himself.

I love the disparity of these people who join me. I probably travel the furthest but there are trainers, non-pros, beginners, competitive youth and retirees, all hauling some distance to ride. It was this group and this teacher who brought me back from the dark and cheerless land of my illness. Riding with them, gingerly and bumbling at first, is what made me know that I'd be fine.

These diverse people are riding brilliant horses that most likely cost in the mid-five figures. Among them are also trail riding, cutting and barrel horses getting some solid schooling, a few futurity colts and always, the up 'n' coming Keystone stars.

I say this tongue in cheek because over the years, I've shown up on some doozies. Even now, remembering them, I have the grace to blush. There were ponies I needed roller skates on to clear the arena floor, others like Amy, Arthur and Tom, who just hauled in for experience but were too small for me to ride. Another kicked out with whoopee cushion special effects for close to a year, every single time I asked for a canter. That was the lovely Pepper.

Some were so overweight that I had to ride them bareback after all the serious riders went home. I couldn't bear anyone watching as I wallowed around on Ray and Black Jack, then Chica. Another just couldn't lope the wide turn around the end of the arena without stumbling into the wall. Bless you, Betty, you kept trying until you could.

One was so shocked and amazed at the overhead lights that he stood, stock still and staring, for an entire lesson, as though seeing angels on high. Winchester, I still smile when I think of this.

One was so brilliant in his reined work and flying changes but was never once able to go by the Coke machine without terror. Yep, that was Eddie. There are still marks on the arena wall — and the side of our trailer — where the now-famous Nelly sharpened her teeth, back and forth, back and forth, like a carving knife.

Some, like Doll, were beyond humbling as I white-knuckled it through those hours, saying little prayers and working my one-rein stops. A few never got the chance to learn the skills they needed because of life's little tragedies. Riel, July and Rockabilly, by God we tried.

Some carried me around in unaccustomed splendour — the pleasant hours spent rocking along on Henry, Johnny, Annie and Tee. Others grew their own fan clubs and would have signed autographs if only their hooves had allowed, the likes of Parry and Prince Charlie.

And now, another year, another horse. Just trying to get a better handle on him before we head out over the open hills come spring. This time, I'm with Pilot. He is making it known that he's upset with these plans of mine.

Our first group lesson, he mostly just pooped and peed. The next lesson, I remember only a lot of kicking up at my leg, along with his gnashing teeth.

Today, Pi's third trip to town, he was starting to figure it out. He walked off the trailer and stood quietly in the parking lot, nostrils wide, drinking in the wind. He sidled up to the 'old lady' step stool for me to mount, smoothly opened and shut the arena gate, started to get a feel for his turnarounds and then, just settled in to the lope. With every minute, I felt him getting a little better, a little more broke.

Pi's going to be some horse. This was the day of the defining moment, that split second that keeps me coming back for more.

Days I'm bored and itching to bust out all over, I'll put on the kettle, make a pot of tea ... and clean some tack. Yes!

I do it the old way, maybe with some opera playing to keep me company. I'll have a big, soft cloth moistened with warm water and I'll use this to make sure the leather is completely clean. Then, a brushing on of some warmed peanut oil if the leather is really dry, or a deep conditioning with my favourite dressing. I rub this in with my fingers, until the saddle or bridle is feeling loved again, 'til it has a good hand. You'll know what I mean when you feel it, as the leather comes alive again. Bits will be washed, silver polished, then all are reassembled and hung on their hooks to be admired.

All the while I'm doing this, I'm thinking of the people and horses long gone to me, the days that were especially bright, memories that lie just below the surface of my here and now but are there to grace my life, the moment I stop and take time to remember them. Cleaning tack is a favourite meditation. I'm feeling better already, aren't you?

English or Western, our horses are all trained with three zones for the rider's leg aids. Any problems with leads, canter transitions and reining-back most often occur because the rider is blurring these. It's simple: the home position has the stirrup leathers hanging vertically, with the rider's ankle just back of the cinch or girth. This area asks for forward impulsion and a basic side pass, for example.

The zone just ahead of our home position asks for lateral movement on the front end, or if both legs are pulsed just slightly toward the girth, will produce either a correct halt or a lively, two-beat reinback (with little use of the hands). Horses resistant at reining back are usually being pulled upon while our legs are still in the home (move forward) position. The 'resistant' horses are in fact right, as this is how we ask for a square halt!

A leg used farther behind the girth in combination with an opposing leg at home is asking for lateral movement of the haunches, including canter transitions and for a change of lead. Degrees of this mean the difference between asking for a turnaround or a beautiful lope departure.

An animal that isn't swinging through the walk is often being ridden with the rider using the legs too far back and/or squeezing them simultaneously. Remember, the energizing zone along the horse's midriff is at or just slightly behind the girth and our legs must echo the alternating motion of the horse.

Green horses have very distinct zones along their barrels, to clarify their understanding of our aids. As they progress in their training, however, our job is to refine these areas and make our cues ever more subtle. Correctly done, the changing leg positions will be felt by the horse or pony, while not so easily detected by an observer.

Whenever we find a horse who's muddling through something he should know, our first thought must be to ensure we're asking clearly with each leg in the appropriate zone. When the pilot error is taken care of, the problem is usually solved.

"All I really needed to know about horses, I learned in high school …" (With apologies to author Robert Fulghum).

Remember the mean girls in high school? For some reason, everyone wanted to be with them, to be like them, even when they got beat up emotionally. I was thinking of my school days as I walked in from gathering the herd. How do you catch many horses in one easy trip? Well, you hang your rope on the 'coolest kid', generally the queen mare in the herd. Everyone else wants to be like her, or at least be with her, so they mindlessly follow her in.

Got a herdbound horse? Once again, the pack mentality comes into play. I shake my head when I see so many people haul a travelling buddy with an insecure one to the veterinarian, or to his first horse show. You be his herd. He's dying for someone to be the cool cat, to show him what to think and do. It will either be you, my friend, or else his buddy back at the trailer. You decide.

The flip side of this scenario is teaching a frightened horse to cross water or learn about traffic or start the lope or learn to drive. If he's got an older, well-schooled horse to 'copy', much of your teaching is done for you. The difference here is we're trying to instill a specific behaviour — and kids pay attention to other kids. This mentorship is so strong that when we're rehabilitating the spoiled, troubled fellow, we make sure that he's with older, well-broke, mentally stable horses only.

Horses and ponies exhibit the same stark social skills, the same brutal pecking order we all survived in high school. Give thanks for the 'years of darkness' — and put 'em to good use.

Submission. Lightness. Relaxation. Three words that sum up our basic horsemanship goals, no matter our equine sport.

Before I climb on any horse — and especially on a new one — I'll pick up the reins and take a soft feel. In mere seconds, her reaction tells me a lot about her mindset and her education. This is a little test I do, just to see if the pony is accepting the bit, or whether we need to do more suppling. I can see if the jaws are soft and the animal is ready to work towards the bit.

When I pick up the reins on an unknown pony, I can quickly see if it has a 'made' mouth or not and proceed accordingly. Most times, this one small step will save us from being reared over on. It's just a good habit to get into, no matter what kind of bit is on the horse.

Do I tie the head in position? Never! This will only teach the horse to lean on the bit or overbend, two outcomes to be avoided at all cost. Lightness only comes when I teach her to move forward and reach towards the bit, something she can never do while standing still.

One of the basic tenets in our program is to teach the horses and ponies, whether ridden or driven, to stand still. This is a skill that once put at the top of your training agenda will quickly improve.

The very first thing we notice with horses that won't wait, or stand still for mounting, is that they are often operating within blurred parameters in their unmounted activities, too. Often, they'll move around just that little bit, just enough that we get used to them and they're never called on it. Time to stage an intervention.

While there are many methods of teaching the whoa word, whether it's using the flag, or moving the horse's feet, or simply calling for quiet insistence, we've found that the key concept is awareness of how much the horse moves around in other areas of our relationship. Once he is standing completely motionless on the cross ties or just with the halter rope thrown over our arm, it's simply a matter of time, adding seconds and minutes to what we ask of him. It's mindful practice.

The reward for absolute stillness is a kind word, then a total release of pressure. I won't touch or even look at the horse but will soften my posture and work on my breathing. Standing then becomes our safe place.

It must be noted that smaller or younger horses will need locking in place to brace against a mounting rider. I'll reach up and push-pull the saddle horn until they get their front legs set, in a widened stance. What a difference this makes. Often, when we blame horses for moving off, they're just getting their balance when we pull on them. They'll stagger a step or two, then momentum just keeps them trucking on ahead.

All our horses are comfortable being mounted from either side. It's a safety feature. That said, they all seem to prefer my using the mounting block or the trailer fender and I respect their choices. They know when they feel good.

There are two key things in this mounting gig. The first, we tend to spend all of five seconds mounting and dismounting with each ride! My response to that is to get the horse set and then mount / dismount / mount / dismount a dozen or more times until the horse gets the picture. This is huge.

Secondly, I see a lot of riders failing to grab some mane in with the rein hand, right tight into the crest. This not only alleviates a huge amount of pull sideways on the saddle, but pulling on the mane this way naturally asks the horse to arch his neck and pull back by locking his legs. Voila! He instinctively puts himself in park and helps us up.

Finally, when we do climb aboard, we never just ride off. This is when my husband used to dig in his pocket for his cigarettes, choosing one, lighting it and putting things away again, revelling in that first deep drag. His horses always went quickly from foot-stomping exasperation to surrender.

Now that he's stopped smoking, we must remind ourselves to settle in the saddle, find our gloves, organize reins, tidy the mane, flex the horse one way, then the other, sit still and think about life. Then, we might back him up, or turn him in a different direction before moving off. I'm always slow to get working: just walking him out, getting the soft feel, asking the horse to stretch and relax.

Magical fixes? Sorry, no. But this approach is doable in mere seconds, doesn't need as much timing and feel as some methods — and has lasting results.

Over the years, we've learned that all horses aren't good ones; all ponies aren't evil. Big or little, they will meet our expectations, however high or low the bar is set.

In my life, I seem to get just what I need. As many of you already know, I am fortunate to be living this dream of training and selling good horses and ponies. Many times, I could do better than I do, whether because of impatience, temper, sloth or greed. None of it matters. Doll crossed my path at a good time. Instinctively, I knew if I wanted to get egotistical and declare war with her, she had many hills she was prepared to die on.

Since this time last year, I have been working and praying for some sign of improvement with this talented ten-year-old mare, picking myself up, dusting myself off and trying, over and over again. Oh, the sleepless nights! Last week, finally, a glimmer of hope for the two of us. This week, though small and insignificant in the grand scheme of things, a victory. It is sweet and I am moved by the mare's generosity. It is another lesson learned.

Running around in circles? Never. Perhaps it's because we work with smaller horses, or perhaps we're just lazy, but we do a lot more lungeing than most western folks do. We use it mainly to teach the pony to carry himself correctly at the walk, trot and lope — without the added burden of a rider.

In a perfect world, our horse or pony will be wearing a light cavesson with a central ring on the noseband. We prefer this to using halter or bridle because it keeps the horse straight. There will be no side reins, no checking or 'setting' the head.

Our animals are known for their beautiful self-carriage, a state of grace that never comes from any other means than allowing the animal to relax and to find his natural balance, to carry his head comfortably where the good Lord intended. Only when the topline has learned to stretch to its utmost, will the pony find his 'swing'. Later on, he'll happily offer to carry himself vertically, without any help from the rider or see-saw reminders on the reins.

Yesterday, Charlie learned to lunge in the round pen. Over-reactive, he'd spooked at the lunge line and galloped 'round like a mad thing. I simply followed him and waited. I was watching for one thing — the stretching that occurs when the thinking side of the brain kicks in. When he did this, we quit for the day, teaching him to settle quickly without those habitual long warm ups.

As in all big journeys, it starts with that hard first step. Fat, dodgy and willful now, he will become a champion.

Mares.

Love 'em or leave 'em, you've gotta know what makes 'em tick. I liken my gals to middle-aged women; they hate to be micro-managed and they don't do stupid. This means you've got to handle them with affection, appreciation and smarts. You have to teach a mare well enough that she knows her job without being nagged on.

The vast majority of mares chug along in faithful service, changing little in their moods or with the seasons. But if your mare isn't among these, if she changes entirely when she's in heat, you have choices.

Have her thoroughly vetted and chiro'd. Don't ride her when she's on the fight. Try feeding raspberry leaves and other remedies. If her back is tender, bring out the Bute. Put on your rubber gloves and put her on hormones. Have her marbled, a veterinary procedure where an intrauterine marble is placed in the mare's uterus, while she is still in heat. The glass ball causes production of progesterone, which can keep a mare from cycling. If that doesn't work and she's worth it, consider having her spayed. This last drastic measure is an unpopular one, yet it morphed my friend's monster — I mean, mare — into a consistently solid horse.

If your mare is never much fun, I hate to say it, but the problem might lie with her training, rather than with her hormones. If her health care team can't find any issues, you might need to get 'er better broke. Whatever you do, please don't breed her just because she needs a job.

If we were to break horses down to two general types, we'd find the 'push-rides' versus the 'pull types' or as my friend Laurie says, those that are 'self-propelled'.

One of these groups is NOT better than the other. Depending on your confidence level and the job you have for your horse, one or the other will just naturally be an easier fit.

The push-ride is the one whose favourite speed is standing still. He'll stop if you quit riding. While many people favour this sort of horse, a lot depends on your own innate qualities. A bolder rider, or even one with waning strength or energy, often gets along better with the self-propelled horse, the one that once put into second or third gear, will still be chugging along at the same speed an hour later.

Self-propelled horses do not necessarily mean hot, high energy horses — although they can be if not thoughtfully trained. Often, we'll choose the push-ride horse, thinking he is safer, but we need to know that he is really broke and not just sleepy. There's a big difference, should he be rudely awakened. Just know that there are comforting and challenging aspects to riding both types.

Bottom line, most nervous riders are best on push-ride horses. It builds confidence knowing that if worse comes to worst, your horse will stop if you quit riding.

Learning what kind of horse you might prefer is easy. Imagine which would be worse — to lose the use of your arms, or your legs, while riding in an arena? Would you hate that you couldn't get going or would you hate that you couldn't stop? Your response will tell you a lot.

Grandad called it 'barn sour' — a horse's reluctance to leave secure surroundings and the inevitable race to get back again. Unwittingly, we can build this vice into a horse that has never before been a problem. By working or schooling and immediately being turned out again, a horse doesn't get the decompression time to process what she's learned. She simply runs off with The Wild Bunch and bingo! We've lost all our good work.

If we're mindful, we can get the training to stick by making the horse comfy, then leaving her to contemplate, or soak if you want a catchy term. This practice, for fifteen minutes to an hour or so, will ramp up her learning and create a calmer, more compliant horse. She will simply stand alone until she stops reacting and starts to relax.

In cooler weather, our horse's warm back would be covered with a rug and she'd be tied in the sunshine, out of the wind. In summer's heat, we'd find her a nice bit of shade. It's not meant to be punishment, just a quiet time and place in which to think.

When I turn my horse out after a ride, I am always mindful of what he's telling me. If he burns off to his friends, bucking and kicking, he's a bit rebellious. If he just turns away morosely, he's feeling sad and used. One that nips or rubs on me is showing a sense of superiority I'm not comfortable with. But on a good day, I'll remove the halter and he'll stand around to chat, head down, relaxed and humble, while I straighten his forelock and tell him he's smart and good. After enough flattery, he'll roll nearby, go for a drink or some salt, then quietly wander off.

Not all days go well. If I've been impatient or rough or demanding, his demeanour when I no longer have any control over him will speak volumes. Sometimes, when remaking spoiled ponies or during tough working days that have forced us over too many hard miles, we can't avoid physical or emotional hurt. But these days should be rare ones.

We know in our hearts when we've treated someone badly. Day after day of mashing on a horse or pony to achieve our goals isn't horsemanship. If this is us, we need to say sorry and do all we can to make the next ride right.

One of my tasks this winter was to book the trailer in for a safety inspection. I'm adamant about doing this on an annual basis but I hated to tie the old girl up for a week during our glorious fall, choosing to leave it for a cold weather job.

High-mileage haulers will need semi-annuals but most of us are playing it safe by getting an expert overhaul on our rigs once a year. The industry standard is having a safety done every 10,000 km (5,000+ miles), which easily adds up if we're on the road a lot. So just what are we wanting done?

An undercarriage inspection is geared for all those hidden but essential areas that are hard to see: tire wear and pressure, regular rotation and lug nuts; brakes; bearings, seals and axles; trailer lights, plug and wiring; breakaway battery and chains; structural safety of undercarriage and hitch, along with the health of floorboards and mats; hinges, latches, other hardware and working locks; any other items that have been worn or damaged, including tie rings, windows, vents, all the stuff that gets wear and tear.

For peace of mind, the actual cost of the inspection — usually under two hundred bucks — is money well spent. Any repairs needed will obviously be added to that. Just know that the value that a well-maintained, used horse trailer holds is worth the cost of upkeep.

Doing this one thing will help to ensure the safety of yourself, your precious horses and your fellow travellers on the road this year. Book a safety inspection today.

Horse people often fall into two groups: the ones who refuse to take any lessons and the ones who can't or won't ride without the coach. While the second group seems to be ever growing, let's delve into the first ...

Riders who are learning-resistant will either say they're nervous to ride in front of a teacher, that they're not skilled enough, or that they've been riding since the discovery of fire and are good, thanks. No, let me rephrase that. We horse people are fundamentally against being told anything; we like the idea of learning but we hate the being taught! Ego is the biggest obstacle to education and yep, most of us constantly need to check our Big E at the door. While my fondest fantasy is of being told I'm too talented to waste my pesos on lessons, that I already know it all, it's not going to happen.

A good teacher isn't afraid of hurting our feelings in order to have us improve... but a good teacher will do this without destroying us. It takes a certain amount of trust to let learning happen and despite best intentions, sometimes we cry all the way home. This, too, shall pass.

If you are frightened to sign up for lessons, you maybe haven't found the right teacher. I urge you to keep trying. If there is no qualified professional in your neck of the woods, a group of like-minded riders can organize a series of clinics throughout the year to share the cost of bringing in someone good.

Whenever I sell horses, I encourage the buyers to get right into lessons to optimize their chances of success. Even then, few buyers will do so, preferring to go it on their own, knowing that if it doesn't work out, they can always return the horse. I struggle with their acceptance of the idea that failure is more welcome than being taught.

Learning-resistant riders make interesting parents. "If it was good enough then, it's good enough now ..." "Our family ranches ..." "I only trail ride ..." "My grandpa said …" "I rode forever without needing lessons …" This common theme keeps a lot of neat little kids from achieving, particularly in Pony Club and 4-H. These tend to be the people who proudly watch their children struggle endlessly with spoiled horses, maintaining that the kids on good horses aren't learning as much. Parents, riding is probably the one area where we don't know what's best for our kids.

Bottom line, find a mentor, even if you yourself are a teacher or have ridden for years. Allow your horsey children to benefit from someone else's teaching. Soak up one good program until it 'sticks' before moving on to the next. Listen during lessons. Write the golden moments down in a notebook when you get home. Learn to put your lessons into practice when you ride on your own. You can do this.

Now, we'll discuss the rider who can't or won't ride without their coach. For various reasons, this type of rider is on the upswing.

I talked to one of these gals not long ago and on threat of death if I leaked her identity, she shared that the taking of lessons, of really getting involved in one program can be a slippery slope. Her previous teacher would get very angry if she went and did anything on her own and that included hacking out, let alone going to competitions. For the first time in her life, this experienced rider began doubting her own abilities to warm up, get to the ring on time, learn her test and problem solve.

The next teacher, while not so strict, had a litany of drills for her to perfect, to work on in her own time. She began to rely on these drills, always feeling in need of the teacher to choose which drills to keep her on track. Things went along until she 'outgrew' her gentle horse and needed one with more talent.

Enter the Superhorse, a young star purchased from a bigger barn, a name-worthy teacher's program and well, you know the rest. Feeling that she is borrowing someone else's property — but still making loan payments to buy it — she knows all too well that there's a real need for her to be kept safe under more knowledgeable hands. Realistically, her young horse has to be maintained by the teacher for lengthy periods of time just to stay on the rails. It gets expensive and in her desire to be a competitive amateur, some of the joy has gone.

There are many different reasons to fear riding without a teacher: fear of messing up in public; fear of surviving the warm-up ring pecking order without a 'barn' to back you up; fear of ruining a professionally made horse; fear of not having the teacher to prep him; fear of not being able to dissect a course or pattern, or strategizing how to ride it ... Some riders don't know how to get their horse to the show grounds, set up a stall, get show ring ready or warmed up without the teacher; others might lack confidence in safely tacking up on their own.

If these sound familiar, it might be time to share your feelings; most coaches want to help. Bear in mind that many amateur riders want everything looked after for them, so that they can just show up and ride.

Do you have any experience with a fear of riding or showing without your mentor? If so, how did you meet it head on?

Hot for teacher ...

A discussion on riding instruction would be incomplete without the sex talk. Yep, we're crossing that line. During the nearly five decades I've been involved in taking lessons and teaching, I've seen that many women prefer male teachers. They flirt, they fantasize and they wouldn't dream of arguing with their guru.

Have a woman show up with the same credentials and watch their enthusiasm drain through the floor. I'm not sure why this is — whether we're brought up to respect the Marlborough Man and/or question womanly skills and knowledge — but it's out there.

Men, as well, need to be faced with an extremely accomplished female instructor before they will take her seriously. Both men and women will accept a bullying approach from male teachers that they will not brook should the instructor be female. This is a fascinating look at the human psyche and is certainly nothing new.

Knowing that men and women have inherently differing teaching and learning styles can actually help us when looking for a teacher. If you have feelings of insecurity or inexplicable fear issues, looking for a woman to teach you is often a better fit. That's the fun part; now, for the darker side.

Twice in my life, I've been faced with wondering why all the teenage girls in our youth program suddenly wanted to quit. In the midst of their mutiny, it came to light that the male teacher was being a tad inappropriate. Something needed to be done. Of course, this does not apply to good and emotionally mature men but it fits a disturbing number of those within the horse industry.

If men are coaching teenage girls, a trustworthy, older chaperone is a must in having the girls feel safe. Yes, I know what year this is. At some point, I'd like to think that each of us will find the teacher we really need, regardless of which way we button our shirts.

I would hazard a guess that most horse wrecks happen due to our own inattention. For one split second, a lapse in our focus means we don't see that the horse is warning us he is bothered, or that our gear is set to malfunction. Driving-horse mishaps also follow this rule.

Tom Jones and I had a near miss the other day and it was entirely preventable, entirely my fault. For some reason, when I was fastening the outer surcingle on his harness — a set I've seldom used and frankly, one that didn't fit him that well — I was careless. I didn't notice that the sewn keeper on the surcingle, the big strap that holds the shaft loops steady, was caught on another loop under the belly band. When I went to fasten the buckle, it appeared comfortably snug but it was in fact about eight inches away from being so.

If I'd been paying attention, I would have seen that it was hanging loose at his offside elbow and I would have noticed that it was buckling far larger than it usually does ... but I was distracted, kind of in a hurry, so I did not see.

Minutes into our drive, bowling along at a spanking trot, the cart wheels dipped into a rut, the shafts flipped up and the loose surcingle goosed the pony violently. The shafts slammed back down, Tom started to buck, he got goosed again and that's when things got interesting. Lucky for me, there was a wire fence nearby and I ran the frightened pony up against it. Lucky for me, he wasn't too scared to see that fence and stop.

I sat there, talking us both down off the ledge, looking over my outfit and wondering what the heck had just happened. Closer inspection showed where

I had made my error. I pulled the surcingle up to its usual fit, so that the shafts would no longer be able to tip up and slam down and as I did so, I was reminded of my late father. His first remark would have been, "Harness never lets you down in a good spot" and his second would have been, "If they want to run away, they'd better be pulling something heavy." Even from the hereafter, my dad's advice was sound.

Tom and I cautiously made it back to the yard, unhitched, let out the traces, found a singletree and hooked up to the old iron harrow. My jumpy, frightened pony then worked off his adrenaline rush by doing a job that requires a lot of physical effort, but it's also a job he does well.

I kicked myself for putting him in this situation but also thanked my lucky stars that his was the sort of personality to get scared, get stopped and to find forgiveness. I've learned the hard way that not all are so blessed.

This ability to shrug it off, to get back in the game, is an essential ingredient in an honest horse. In the name of safety and building confidence, we must be so very careful. Sadly, until we've gone with a green one into a tough situation and made it out the other side, we've no real idea of the depth to his character. I now know more about Tom than I'd bargained for. Thankfully, it's all good.

In-hand work.

I'm asked about it often. There's a magic to it, when well done, an opportunity to get beyond the bump and grind of ridden work by rehabilitating and reshaping the questionable areas — mental and physical — on any horse. There is an increasing number of people who've replaced all thought of riding with only in-hand work. I am not among them. Not yet.

This last decade, after a life-changing illness and the requisite hours spent riding my bed, I've become an earnest student of lungeing — of working a horse from beside him, rather than from the top. While recuperating my own body, I could also get my horse ready to ride. Working in hand, lungeing various circles, straight lines, even lateral movement is of practical use, as so many of the ponies in my care are actually too small for me. It stands to reason that the more I can accomplish with balance and straightening from the ground, the better they'll be equipped to do their jobs.

Older performance horses, in particular, can rebuild toplines and strengthen areas of their bodies that have been eroded with less than ideal work. They learn to stretch and balance and carry themselves without relying on the reins or dealing with a rider. Soon, I watch them again find joy in their movement, a state of grace that is all too often lost.

With my own horses, I delve into these teachings whenever they (or I) feel fragile or somehow despairing. These are well-loved tools in my tool box. Always, though, I need to remember the people I am serving. Will the hours spent in-hand benefit the child who rides one of my horses into the rodeo arena or the one piloting her pony 'round a jump course? To some degree, yes. But to meet these demands, I know of no way around taking time and making miles.

Honouring the notion that my training must have the goal of bettering my horses' minds and bodies, I've decided that in-hand work is a 'go with' to my program — but not an 'instead of'.

What is the difference between working in hand on the lunge and round penning? For me, these are two entirely different realms.

In the first, the horse learns to balance between my hand and my forward intent. This is a very close approximation of the balance while we're riding. In round penning, I am establishing a balance between moving away from me and staying close. As such, round penning is an excellent way to build trust while establishing submission.

Lungeing is a closer approximation of how I want my horse to work while I am riding or driving. I will do this by encouraging him, through a giving contact on the lunge rein, asking him to bend, to stretch the area in front of his withers and through his gullet. I will ask him to step forward with swing. I can observe his tail, his chewing response, his rhythm. As he starts to relax and stretch down through the topline, his throat will actually start to bounce up and down as he trots. This is good.

I have learned that when I am awash with endorphins myself, watching my horse with pleasure, I know that he will be working to the best of his ability. It's all a matter of energy.

The gear that I use is very important in the outcome of lungeing. I am using a light cavesson with a central ring on the nose. I do not use a riding bridle with a bit attached, or even a regular halter. No matter how well adjusted, these will pull crooked and in turn, make my horse crooked and heavy in the hand. Both directions of the horse receive the same attention and the horse is worked at all paces, walk, trot and canter, because each of these gaits brings its own good medicine.

Most importantly, I use no side reins. I use no reins tied to the saddle or behind the cantle. I use nothing to influence the horse other than his own forward movement and his will to stretch. It's a bit like yoga, as compared to pumping iron.

NOTES

NOTES

NOTES

SPRING
Wellness

We've made it! Oh, these evenings of long, golden sunrays, seeing soft green upon the trees. Horse hair is flying everywhere and we're itching to get back in the saddle. Some of us may have ridden all winter — if it is our job on the ranch, or if we have access to heated places — but many of us have not. We've got to get back in the game.

Many of us face this alone. A fresh horse and muddy, slippery ground can be daunting. I've learned that a step-by-step approach works well for reminding my horse that I do play an important part in its life, that last year's same ol' rules apply. I have a plan in place for establishing these ground rules. This is the time of year to work methodically through them, at a pace of our own that feels right.

Spring is about mentorship. We search for the teachers and role models who share our core values, those who will stretch us into achieving more than we might on our own. Good mentors are treasures and throughout my life, I've had several. These wise people have helped me deal with disappointment, along with any healing or learning needed to rise above my past. These people are blessings ... and as the grass greens and the songbirds return to our pastures, they steer us along safer paths.

Here's to our own health and wellness! Let's get stronger and find more joy in all that we know and what we have yet to learn. Spring is the time of growth and abundance. For us to mentor our own horses, our thoughts and changes must come from within.

MENTORSHIP

Every so often, I check in with a counsellor who I now consider a trusted friend.

She uses a phrase that really sticks with me. "Everything we do comes down to healthy boundaries," she says. From handling the boss at work who pushes too hard, the friend who treats us badly, the gossipy neighbour who phones too early and too often, this is sage advice.

If we learn to build our virtual fences — and then maintain them — we don't have to overreact and wage war whenever openings are breached. You know, whenever our feelings get hurt.

Horses are very good at keeping boundaries. We might work them too hard and they'll withdraw by shunning the treat we bring, or by growing hard to catch. We perhaps get too competitive, at their expense, and they simply tell us. Straight off.

By communicating our misdemeanours clearly, without personal insult, they let us know that we've done wrong. When it comes to our teachers, our horses rank among the best.

Dear Parent:

Take heed with how you mount your child. If you wish her a lifetime of joy in the saddle, those first ponies will either make or break your dreams. A kind and sensitive pony makes a kind and sensitive rider. When defensive parents argue that kids who learn to ride on good horses can only ride good horses, I just shake my head. Learning to ride well on a good 'un is hard enough — kids shouldn't have to struggle with any other kind.

When you buy a pony for your small child, you are buying the most important horse of her lifetime. She must be safe, without doubt, but your child ideally will learn the feeling of correct horsemanship, along with a joy and love of riding that will sustain her for life. This is only made possible on a horse or pony that is respectful and experienced — an animal that has worked long and hard to master a job.

For children, riding should be pure joy, something to remember fondly when they look back on childhood. Let's face it. There are enough things in life to cause tears and anxiety; riding should not be among them.

What price safety?

Our children were blessed to start their horsemanship journeys on horses and ponies belonging to their grandparents — animals that had thousands of well-ridden miles under their belts, along with vast stores of horse sense.

We've long realized the beauty of such a relationship — the vulnerable and impressionable youngster atop his wise and well-intentioned horse. We prefer that the age of the child and the age of his mount adds up to at least twenty, or as close as we can make it.

The bottom line? Somebody has to be the brains in the outfit.

In our family, this was Playgirl, a twenty-something gem entrusted with carrying our tiny children all over the ranch. We figured as long as they were on her, with or without us, they wouldn't get into trouble. Playgirl never let her family down and my children were just some of the many people she influenced, through three generations.

I find that starting a horse down the right path is one thing; maintaining a horse so that he is evolving and improving is another. There's an art to keeping a horse going well and a simple thing a lot of people overlook is the power of change. If your horse is a stoic one, if he is starting to feel dull and unresponsive, changing his bits around can work magic.

Sensitive, fussy horses are often comforted by keeping their bitting the same but I find the "yada-yada-whatever" ones are kept fresh with a rotation of maybe three bridles that I'll work through by swapping out every so often. I'll make note of which each prefers — because there's usually one they'll be happiest in — and save that bit mainly for the big days.

Don't worry about staying within your discipline or rules and legalities when you're playing at home. A side pull or pelham or correction bit might be just the change your horse is looking for. Be safe, be realistic — don't put something on a horse that is light years ahead of where he's at today. I also don't change the bit on a kid's horse without riding it first, myself.

Buying bits we don't need can get expensive, so I'm not above asking my friends if I can try one of theirs. Riding clubs and stables might consider starting a bit bank for their membership just for this reason. I'll wash the bits before and after and make sure my horse knows what the bit and chin strap or chain are going to feel like from the ground, first, before I climb aboard. By the way, I never tie my horse's head into position. I just bridle him up a bit, back him up some and let him process the different feel, unmounted. Only then, if all's well, will I step on and ride.

Like changing our shoes midway through a long day on our feet, swapping bits out on our horses can bring new life to them. These little things are worth a try.

Sometimes we'll look at those very quiet ones, and we'll wish, "Oh, wouldn't it be nice if they were more forward, or had more spring in their step, or ... ?" We always need to remember that their greatest gift is their ability to absorb stuff that would drive other horses mad. For me, it's all too easy to start resenting them for the one thing that made me fall in love with them in the first place.

Kind, quiet horses and ponies are the best confidence-builders. Remember, there is no more formidable rider than the child who knows no fear.

I'm often asked why I lope my ponies so much — and why even the youngish ones are packing curb bits.

Yes, I lope 'em a lot, using third gear until it becomes as relaxed and comfortable as walk and trot. With some horses and ponies, that's a lot of loping. The hot ones, especially, need to learn that a lope or a gallop is just another gear before we walk on a loose rein. All the ponies, especially the driving ones, must learn to gallop without running away.

Too many people fail to lope the ponies that will be ridden by little kids. I, for one, don't want my pony loping for the first time when he's startled, with a little passenger on board.

And the curb bits? When that dear pony is sold, folks, he's going to get bitted without my blessing in just about anything. Far better his education in a shanked bit begins with me, rather than with a six-year-old kid at the reins.

Oh, my goodness. One week ago, we wore everything we owned, just to do chores. This morning, the birds were singing up a celebration, I heard the geese nesting along the creek and even though a winter coat was involved, there was coffee on the verandah.

Meanwhile, it occurred to me that with this patch of nice weather, I would take the leg straps off my gelding's turnout rug. I was growing tired of dealing with them, you see. The thought briefly flashed across my mind that if it got windy, I might lose said blanket but gosh, the blue skies were sunny and heck, why was I always such a bloody-minded pessimist?

Fast forward several hours and there was the horse, sans blanket, shivering in the cold. In the end, I'd looked in the pasture for hours and nope, nothing. Funny how every molehill started looking like a navy blue WeatherBeeta ... Guess he'll be rockin' the ol' rugged patch job tonight. By the way, I found the blanket ... a year later.

The biggest ongoing problem you'll have with any kids' horse is in keeping it good. Too often, the child is mounted up and wished bon voyage — and then we wonder what's happened when everything starts heading south.

What's the answer? You've gotta run interference. Let's face it. Kids aren't big on commitment or follow through. You, or some trustworthy adult, must see that the head toss towards home doesn't turn into full-scale balking, that the blown left lead doesn't become No Left Lead, that the refusal at the little cross rail doesn't escalate into something major. Trust me, these things do — and depending on the animal, a kid's horse or pony can start dialing out over the course of just one or two days.

The answer is to stay involved. Be prepared to buckle up and ride!

A number of us have bought 'broke' horses or ponies for ourselves or the kids… and they're just not working out. Many times, hefty sums were paid and still, we get burned. We're intelligent enough people who truly want what's best for our families, so how can we do better?

This sounds harsh but don't automatically believe what any seller is saying about their horse. We don't have to be argumentative know-it-alls but seeing is believing. If a seller claims that kids can lope around bareback, riding double, then we need to see that being done. If they say they can quietly ride out alone in a stiff wind, they'd better be ready to prove it.

Next, remember those horses or ponies who were saints at age two and everyone grew up together? Forget about 'em, they're rare as unicorns. If we're shopping for kids, our pony and child's ages had better add up to eighteen or twenty.

When we go shopping, the following should be standard equipment for beginner-safe horses, whether for adults or children. We mustn't consider them as options. This list is a basic one and does not include such things as jumping ability or knowing how to swap leads, for instance.

Schooling adds to the value of any horse but from a safety standpoint, never trumps the need for the following in a beginner's horse: ease of catching, tying, loading and unloading; walking, jogging, loping; working in a bit, not a halter; circling and going in straight lines, riding out away from home — alone or in a group; neck reining, useful if we're into English and essential if Western.

We want more whoa than go, with respectful ground manners and handling of feet; allowing jackets to be put on and taken off while mounted; safe riding around dogs, machinery and road traffic; standing still for mounting and a healthy respect for the word whoa.

Any hint of balkiness, herdboundness, crow hopping, spookiness, rearing, biting, shying, halter pulling while tied, or a lack of willingness on the part of the seller to show the animal going under saddle are deal breakers. Can these things be fixed? Maybe, but not in beginner hands.

Remember, seeing is believing. If, for any reason, we cannot watch this stuff happening, we'd best go home with an empty trailer. The bottom line? 'Beginner safe' means a willingness to build confidence and the love of riding. Neither can happen where there is fear.

It's tax time and I've forgotten where I've put my sense of humour. Early morning saw me at the computer, cramming desperately with a lapful of receipts, not quite feeling the spirit of the season. Sitting there, waiting for Mike to join me and explain some of these, waiting, waiting... and the phone rings.

It's him, burbling happily about whether I would mind tromping over the stubble field and help him pull the ton truck out, loaded with a round bale for feeding. I've no idea what the man was thinking, for I was up to the axles myself, just walking out to him.

There was the truck, eighteen inches shorter than usual, with every chain and bungee cord he could find, along with fifty feet of heavy cable snaking from the front of the truck, through a sloughy bit, past a grain bin, then around a ninety degree turn through a wire gate, to the waiting tractor.

"Which end would you like?" he asked generously. Afterwards, while I scraped mud off my face and waited in the warm truck for him to gather up the chains and cable, I was fiddling with the radio dial when an old song I used to like came clear.

"Oh yeah, life goes on, long after the thrill of livin' is gone ..." Pretty much.

Getting one of my horses ready for a trial tomorrow when it suddenly hit me — I'd made a grave omission in his schooling, as seen through the eyes of a child. Quick! Off came the saddle and I managed a graceless flying wallenda onto him from alongside the fence. Jogging, loping, 'round the yard and then down to the creek for a soak, legs akimbo, singing, riding bareback ...

How long has it been since I've had this much fun riding? A timely reminder to stop milking the joy out of life.

What's up with the adult riding the teeny, tiny pony? Isn't it cruel?

Here's the thing — if you haven't ridden your child's horse, or seen it ridden by knowledgeable hands, how do you know it's safe? How do you possibly know what your child is going through, every time he or she climbs aboard? In this instance, we need to know the pony is broke and soft in the bridle at all three gaits before we can recommend him.

Shame on any adult who puts a child up on an unknown or questionable horse or pony — and yet, we see it all the time.

"Where the boys are ..."

One thing's for certain, they're seldom on horseback. It's an issue that equestrian sport is taking seriously because, according to a survey by the British Horse Society in 2015, girls now outrank boys, three to one. I've a hunch this discrepancy is even greater in other parts of the world, depending on the riding discipline. It's certainly obvious at our local clinics and horse shows. If you've a boy in your life who is actively 'horsey' and loving it, he deserves a tip of our hats.

Nothing against us wimminfolk. It simply saddens me that in another generation, we will have so few good men mentoring us in equestrian sport. Besides, there are huge benefits for boys who grow up amongst horses.

If we teach children, we need to prove that we can actually do what we tell them. That old saying, "do as I say and not as I do" is a cop out. If we can't because of age or other infirmity, then we'd better have the pictures to prove it before we teach it.

Parents, if you're asking your child to ride a horse or pony, first make sure that you, yourself, can ride him. If you can't, then you'd best find someone who can because expecting a child to perform a high-risk activity on an untried horse or pony is beyond wrong. In any case, the teacher must make darned sure the pony jumps the jumps and goes and stops and turns, alone and in the group, BEFORE the little student climbs aboard. This is not heroics. It's called due diligence and is something we see too many people gloss over these days.

Maybe my age is colouring my thoughts, but there seem to be more child prodigies now than ever before, certainly since the days I was an ordinary kid. Today's parents are under huge pressure to raise winners — and when they go horse shopping, they're not looking for just any ol' nag.

I've taken to calling these precious babes 'tot stars' — children who, according to their parents, would be at the Olympics, if not for their tender years. It sounds funny until you see them, kind and gentle kids who are doing their best, still loving their time spent with horses, despite constant hectoring and badgering from those in the driver's seat.

"She's been training horses since she could walk." "Her teacher can't believe how far ahead she is for her age." "She won at Shady Grove last week." "He's fearless and we're afraid of buying something that will hold him back." "Deirdre, just ride like it's a regular third level test." And so on. The reality, even if these children could possibly deserve this build up, is that such statements most reflect the self-worth of the parents — and the pressure those little shoulders bear is huge. Many children are overmounted because of being pushed to being something great. It's off-putting to witness and one of the more toxic elements facing young riders today.

I urge you, parents, to simply encourage your children, find them a worthy teacher and a barn 'family' they can be part of, especially if you've been planning to be your child's coach. Paying a worthy mentor will go far in salvaging the parent-child relationship, particularly once your kid becomes a teen. Too often, we see the 'teaching' of family members that, in any other context, would be labelled abuse.

Then, I urge you to find your child a safe and honest pony or horse. Six-year-old riders do not require beauty and raw talent under them.

If the horsemanship they are immersed in is sound, if the atmosphere is good, they will grow into kind and generous people who are team players, able to do their life's work with dedication, never needing false praise or fanfare. Society will provide more than enough pressure. Do not let the burden of your high hopes sit heavily upon your kids.

The flip side of pushing our kids to achieve is in letting them explore. Kids need time with their dreams and innermost thoughts, learning to love a living being other than themselves. These, I think, are the greatest gifts of horsemanship.

There is a common and very sad phenomenon that is particular to the children of horsey and knowledgeable parents. It's the situation where mum and dad want the child to ride "way mo', way bettah" than the child does. This happens without any wish for tension or unhappiness on the parents' part, I think.

Simply put, riding and horsemanship define who and what these families are. Add in the natural tendency among parents for our children to live better lives and reach higher goals than we ever did and it's a recipe for disaster. If you stir a little competitive ego into the brew, it can get downright nasty.

Why am I so sensitive to this scenario? To be honest, I've been that parent.

I've forced my eighteen-month-old to put the chaps on, hold the reins "like an ice cream cone" and led him 'round the show ring. I've made the little kid ride the high-powered pony that was too much horse. I've made the teenagers go to the shows every weekend, lope endless circles while I critiqued, when they might have liked some time to just swim in the creek with their friends. Worse, I've made the keen, keen child cry all the way home because I thought she could have ridden better at the big show. Oh, the shame.

So, here's the thing. Those of us who love horses probably all wish that our children might learn to love riding. When we dream these incredible dreams for them, however, we need to make darned sure these are their dreams, too. Otherwise, it all becomes a nightmare that taints the relationship with our children for years to come, long after those wins are forgotten.

Mentorship: what's healthy, what's necessary, what keeps us from moving ahead? Let's take it a step further and talk about the people you choose to guide and shape your kids.

When you pick a teacher for your child, choose wisely. This person is not only sharing his, or her, knowledge on riding but also how to live: how to treat other people, how to be a steward amongst the animals, how to hold oneself with dignity and compassion, how to tread lightly upon this earth.

In the great game of horsemanship, there are many diverse players. When picking a teacher for your child, choose with your heart as well as your head.

Have I mentioned that I began teaching 4-H when I was all of seventeen? My new boyfriend's parents had just started a light horse club and wouldn't it be fun if the ranch kids in the group could enjoy some culture — that is, English lessons? Obviously, they had not got input from the ranch kids, whose singular aspiration was rodeo glory over at the bucking chutes.

The prickly issue of dwindling attendance in my English class was cleverly dealt a blow when the leader decreed that Rodeo Club kids had to take Western and English Horsemanship, as well. This long chapter of my life is but another reason I am grey haired and twitchy. For me, 4-H will always be 'the best of times and the worst of times', all in one.

But just when it would appear hopeless, Achievement Day would dawn in June. The kids and horses would be scrubbed and shining, whipcord breeches and leather gaiters pulled from ancestral trunks and somehow, somehow, the horses had learned their leads, the kids had learned their diagonals and a peculiar air of triumph and mothballs would enfold us.

So, they'd been listening. I would be moved to tears of pride while the judge awarded the ribbons. We would lunch on beans 'n' wieners washed down with Tang, heartfelt and sticky hugs were shared and then, for another year, it was done.

The horse or pony that is good enough to help raise your child is, in the overall horse population, a rarity. The one that can take your child all the way from leadline, through walk-trot, all the levels of Pony Club or 4-H, then to the highest competition your teenaged child can aspire to is almost mythical. Every now and then, we find one — but it's very, very seldom that we do.

This means that most of us who go on to be 'serious' riders will have been carried by several different ponies and horses. Some will give courage, some will give the thrill of victory, others, the sting of disappointment. Each of these horses will teach us something valuable. This is as it should be.

Often, I talk to parents who want the one animal that will do it all. I understand the financial and emotional implications of 'step up' animals but, provided the outgrown horse or pony is well cared for, well-schooled and sold on to a deserving and fortunate family, it will play a key role in financing your child's next ride. The alternative, of course, is to keep having children so that the beloved pony always has a job!

Remember, a good partner will prepare your child for the next step on his (or her) horsemanship journey. Our ultimate goal is a well-grounded young person, full of gratitude and resolve, ready to face the world.

I would like to emphasize this thought that pertains to the older teens: the training of the young horse is the pinnacle of the young rider's achievement.

This means that everything they have done to this point has been in preparation for sharing their knowledge with a young horse. Waiting and working towards the *gift* of a clean slate horse has been the goal throughout their riding — not simply success in the show ring.

How often do we see young riders made bigger than they ought to be by show ring glory on made horses and it's everything to their happiness? Consequently, kids working on unmade horses feel as though it's not an honour to be training because they are not usually winning.

This is backward thinking; it does not promote an excellence in maturity or horsemanship.

Yes, the young rider needs to build competence for a number of years on an excellent horse but the goal is to eventually attain the knowledge and confidence to take it a step further with a project. Thus, the show ring becomes the means to betterment, not an end.

Our young rider learns that being judged, that someone else's opinion, is just one way of monitoring progress and is not a measure of their own self-worth. Learning that good comes from dedicated work and not from pressing a button, learning that success is an up and down journey and not a straight climb ... all are valuable life lessons.

Outside help and encouragement will be there in the form of mentorship, which is as it should be. A caution: when choosing your teen's riding teacher, you are also choosing a model of character and kindness, so choose wisely.

Can horsemanship help our teenaged children grow into balanced and healthy adults? In a word, yes.

Going it alone, or, getting by without a mentor.

I'm a true believer in the power of mentorship. That no matter where we may be on this journey, whether just starting out or nearing the end, that there be someone to guide us, to accept our vulnerabilities, to hold our feet to the fire whenever we go wrong. A mentor will keep one true to tradition, saving us from wildly fish-tailing through one fad to the next.

Finally, anyone in the horse business needs to have done the work, the hard stuff, under somebody worthy before they go out on their own. Whether fixing problem horses or running an office, there's no need to reinvent the wheel when we can learn from someone who's already made the same mistakes.

That said, there comes a time when you need to stand up on your own rather than endlessly be told what to do and think. It's all too easy to be in lessons for a lifetime without taking the responsibility for making them stick. While we all benefit from a pair of eyes on the ground, the learning to ride by feel — the learning to problem solve and know just what is needed and when — is powerful stuff.

Do we need to put a little pressure on to progress? Where is the timing in our release? Either way, how much is too much? How little is not enough? Does the horse need more work in one particular area? Or less? So much depends on our horses and so much depends on us. Are we active and a bit more 'go for it' in our approach or are we passive and introspective? One will have as much influence as the other. A goal when we train alone might be to seek and recognize this fine balance.

Going without our mentor, even going longer between lessons, is one sure fire way to find out.

I drove a school bus for many, many years. Without realizing it, I began to put the kids under my care into two separate groups: those with animals in their lives and those without. I know, this seems harsh and unfair. But wait.

The kids with animals — anything they considered pets, really — had a gentleness about them, a wisdom that went beyond their years. I would pick them up in the morning and there would be excited stories of new adventures and other times, there would be the most awful tears. Oh, the inevitable heartbreak.

But they were the lucky ones, because the kids without had something vital missing from their lives. Often, they didn't seem to know quite how to go about touching other living beings, or how to worry about someone separate from themselves. Having a pet was almost like learning how to parent.

It made me think that this grind of signing up our children for riding lessons, or putting them in obedience classes with the old dog, or driving them to the local shelter to volunteer, is for a greater purpose than what we might imagine as we wait in the parking lot, with another cold coffee, on another dark Tuesday night.

When we teach our children to love outside themselves, along with all the risks and hurts, we teach them something that cannot be learned in school, or found online, or read in books.

To those of you struggling to make ends meet, to keep up the shuttle service, to teach the difficult teens, I urge you to keep going. When you teach children about animals, you teach them about life.

A TIME TO HEAL

Fear. I've had a few tastes of it — the runaway Percherons with bits bent backwards they'd pulled so hard, the horse that lost his mind in the trailer, the pony that kicked the hat off my head. But always, sick on adrenaline, I'd breathe "Thank you, God" and keep on keepin' on.

Not this time. It had started out a perfect day, just some friends getting together to drive their horses. We had good people, good horses and equipment and we knew what we were doing. In the end, we witnessed my friend, her horse and carriage in a blind runaway, hitting the wall of the arena so hard the poor horse instantly died. It was caused by an equine aneurysm, something nobody could have foreseen.

The violence and horror of the wreck was certainly nothing that my friend's sweet and gentle horse would have chosen. But as we sat in the hospital waiting room afterward, one of us turned to the other and with pupils dilated breathed, "Only a fool would want to drive a horse." That was back in January.

I should have got over it. Goodness knows, our injured friend bravely did. But those of us who weren't knocked out were not, somehow, quite so lucky. Dread became a familiar lump of something cold and sinister I swallowed every time I had to hitch up. Worse, driving horses had been the one constant in my life, the thing that had always brought me joy.

When people tell you to not be afraid, or to 'show him who's boss', it doesn't help. You can lie to anybody you want, but you can't lie to your horse and you sure can't lie to yourself. All you can do is admit you are by God worried and hope you've got yourself a horse that won't take advantage of that fact. Then, you start healing.

For the past few months, I've flitted back and forth with being brave but the reality is, there are colts to drive, green ponies to get those hairy miles on before they can find new homes. I'm making myself get out there. Little by little, it's getting better. I may even become a more sympathetic teacher, knowing now that fear is not a weakness — it's our old friend Wisdom trying to keep us safe.

And you know what? Last night as I settled into the carriage and picked up my whip, my heart actually soared. I breathed deeply, then I said, "Walk on."

There are many horses working with sore backs. We find that mares, especially, can be sensitive in the lumbar region, whether due to their work loads, their heat cycles or simply, their longer builds.

By watching my horses, I learn when they're feeling frail. One of the ways I get the message is while loading or unloading from the trailer. Often, they'll stop halfway with their front feet up and their hinds down on the ground. I used to tell them to keep moving but not any more. I'll wait — and if they stretch downwards, licking and chewing, I know they crave the chance to stretch their toplines. On the other hand, if they look back over their shoulders or heaven forbid, root with their noses, they're just pulling my chain.

I have one that will step right in and out when she's feeling fine — but if not, she'll pause halfway for a stretch. She knows I'll allow her to stop with her body on the incline and it's rewarding when I see her lick her lips, drop her head, yawn and sigh. In no way am I suggesting that massage or chiro are not needed. This — along with correct training that allows her to carry me with an upwardly stretched topline — is just something I can do to ease the day. A few moments are all it costs and my horse repays me by working well. It's a fair trade.

I've noticed — more so as I age — that when I step off an unbalanced or slightly unsound horse, I'm sore. I feel tender, fragile, beat up. This is a good thing! It reminds me that I am not on a machine to be made to perform. Rather, I'm on a living, breathing being that is either comfortably working, or isn't.

Hurting after we ride is a helpful reminder that our body's energy mirrors that of our horse. If we are sore — in our hip, in our lower back — I believe that he probably is, as well. It's another tool to keep our riding mindful.

I've been gathering the spoils of years of collecting to be cleaned, priced and put up for sale. I was doing well until I got to the old linens. Some of them were so beautiful, they almost hurt me. The feeling of a piece of real, fine, aged linen has to be experienced to be believed... So lustrous, you want to hold it against your cheek.

Why, you ask, would a modern tomboy like me be so moved when she holds a piece of old handwork? I think, simply, because the story of women holding it all together, stitch by tiny stitch, is a part of all of us. This need to find beauty in the ordinary is maybe in our DNA.

Horses have long been touted as natural healers. This is truly lovely but the reality, when seen from the working animal's point of view, can be something else. Most of the equines I know thrive in an atmosphere of trust, security and sameness. Take away any one of these and the wheels start falling off.

If we are looking for a performance horse or pony, we need to be very honest about the state of our emotional and mental wellness.

According to the statistics, one in every five of us will face some form of mental health issue in our lifetime — anxiety, depression or bipolar disorder, among others. That's twenty percent of us. It goes to follow that some will be horse people.

Our beloved animals are magnets for unspoken emotional stuff — and not all of them are equipped to deal with it. The ability to weather highs, lows and long, dark journeys requires a somewhat stoic horse. Sadly, no amount of training or lessons will make a too-sensitive one more able to cope.

It is a bleak thing when a mismatched horse and rider find themselves trapped in a no-win situation — and nobody seems willing or able to talk about it. I suspect we all have days when we should not go to the barn.

While the outside of a horse is good for the inside of a man, woman or child, if this is a topic close to your heart, please be honest about the kind of horse you need. He's out there — but he's also out of the ordinary. Seek help. Take care. Stay safe.

My spotted mare has hurt herself. Fine one night, she's come home the next morning with a nasty cut on her leg. In addition to science — antibiotics — she is being treated with love and honey and daily soakings in magical warm black tea.

I've been doing one thing wrong, however, and that has to do with my attitude. I schlepped out this morning, down in the dumps and worried and there she was — waiting at the gate in the sunlight, knowing I'm on my way, whinnying a joyful good morning. I'd forgotten that the chance to doctor a beloved horse is a gift that strengthens our bond, a deposit into the gratitude account for a change.

As Doll stands with her sore leg in the bucket, I smooth her mane. She shakes her head and I stroke it pretty ... again and again and again.

Today, I taught a riding lesson to a beautiful bookkeeper and financial advisor who has decided to confront her longstanding fear of horses. As we talked and relaxed afterward over glasses of iced tea, she gently suggested it might be time for me to come face-to-face with my longstanding fear of money.

Old patterns are hard to recognize. They are harder to change and as we talked, I wondered, who was teaching whom, here? It was quite a day.

Perhaps I was naive, or blessed, or just arrogant. I actually believed that nobody in our family could ever get hurt. We practically lived on our horses. They were ours from start to finish. We used good equipment, we rode smart and were careful. We didn't do any of the stupid things I see online. We always, always got by.

Within a span of about ten years, however, enough had happened that a new thing called doubt started creeping in.

Turns out that losing one's nerve isn't a state reserved for beginners. If you've been in the game long enough, you'll see and experience things that seem best left unsaid. So, let's talk about the emotional battering that comes from watching a friend or family member get hurt.

If you've seen someone you love get injured with horses, or have had to care for them in recovery — or buckle your spurs on and fill in the gap, as so often happens when a farm or ranch family member is hurt — don't be surprised or ashamed if you start feeling fearful.

Our reactions can take a year or more before they fester into something big enough to acknowledge. In this case, it helps immeasurably to talk to someone safe and trustworthy about what's going on in one's heart and head. This sharing, alone, can ground us and reassure us, a bit like turning the light on when there's a monster in the closet.

If you've decided that it's key to your spirit to take up where you left off, at some point you'll have to get back in the game. This means caring for yourself by riding and working ONLY with trustworthy people and genuine horses. Aligning ourselves with quality people and animals will rebuild us.

I don't believe that accidents are as simple as getting what we deserve. Often, there's one crystalline moment when everything aligns and something bad happens. Otherwise, it's just another near miss.

Know that there's a difference between recovering from a trauma where everyone's been having fun with high courage, to watching a wreck after days, weeks, months of foreboding. That long, drawn-out stuff can really chip away at the nerves. Most shattering of all is when a child or a mentor gets hurt.

If this is you, I beg you to unload the burden of fear with a confidante. Don't be surprised if this is also accompanied by a sense of shame, for we horse people are supposed to be above all human emotions. Not. Rebuild yourself with a worthy horse, step by step by step. Be gentle and patient, trusting that within each of us is the immense potential to heal.

I've been asked again if I would teach riding lessons. What a loaded question. While I've taught for many years, this is something that puts knots in my stomach and I've never dug down and got to understanding why.

I've loved teaching. Far from teaching because I thought I was great, I taught despite myself. I, as well as anyone, understood the mental and emotional costs of just setting foot into the arena and coming out alive. For four and a half years, I rode, lived and trained with a teacher that most people could only dream of studying under. This was a good thing. But it also allowed me to rationalize the physical, verbal and emotional abuse I endured while in her care. It's taken me over thirty years to have the courage to remember it.

I have been silent and shameful, making secret the wounds worn by both myself and often, the talented horses in her care. Many years later, I can still go long periods of surviving and working, only to lose my temper with a horse if anyone questions my ability or purpose. Control, ego, lies and unspoken violence have always seemed to be just under the surface of my little world.

I'm in a delicate place right now. I want to heal, to help, to give words to what I've carried around within me. Yes, the riding, training, showing and teaching scene is one of victims and offenders. For years, I've believed that kindness was equivalent to weakness; that riding well was about showing who was boss.

My world was centred around people who perpetrated violence on the apprentices and animals entrusted into their care. I have been their student. I now ask forgiveness for my acceptance, for standing silent when I might have spoken out. Right now, I am wading through the heavy water of having lived in something considered glamorous, a place for heroes and winners but was rotten to the core.

If you ask me to teach you, please be patient. Maybe I will. But I'm going to look after myself here, for a while.

Making the time to ride.

It's a lament we cry over and over. Let's face it. By the time we've seen to family, endless chores, careers, homemaking, health and finances, there's little left of us to cope with anything else.

I've learned that if I don't make time to do this one thing I have loved since childhood, something vanishes from my life — and it isn't just barnyard-y laundry. The joy goes ... and despite the high price of getting 'out there', my life without some form of equine involvement is hardly living.

There have been hectic times and years of ill health when my horse fixes came from teaching the odd lesson, volunteering at therapeutic riding or just helping run the out gate at shows. I've tried photographing horses, auditing clinics, even learning to be a scribe. I've packed a picnic lunch and spent the day watching and learning at any equine event I could find. I've signed out every single Billy and Blaze book from the town library. I even watched National Velvet again.

All were good for my soul when I couldn't get real, live saddle time. And if I'm honest, there were years I could've ridden more but didn't. I needed to sign up for lessons and be fired up about learning new skills.

Is it time to honour the horse-crazy child within you? Just asking, 'cause being a 'grown-up' gets old.

You come to a certain age — a certain level of experience — and it becomes harder getting yourself hired, whether you happen to be needing work or a new beginning. This holds true with women, and with horses.

Why? I think the people doing the hiring are looking for that clean slate. Maybe they're holding out for something cheaper, a little easier on the eye, but mostly I think they want an open-minded employee who will just say, "Yes, sir!" and get the job done.

Doll is standing in my line of sight out the dining room window as I write this. (Like planets in orbit, she and I are always aware of the other.) Three geldings would like to leave the feed ground and make the long trek to water. She is not ready. The rising sun has not yet warmed her sides. The boys, too timid to continue without their warrior princess, circle back and wait. An hour or so later, they are waiting on her, still.

Owning a strong-willed mare can be a bit like working with a middle-aged woman. Both have learned much through the school of hard knocks, they can smell a fake a mile off, and they don't do stupid. If you are into micro-management, they will be your constant headache.

Doll is no exception. She can be rock solid; that is, if and when she wants it. She can also reduce me to a blithering idiot with smoke pouring from my ears. The bravest horse I ride, she doesn't mind turning broncy if it suits her. Every upward transition is accompanied by a swish of the tail, as in 'I read you loud and clear, moron'. She gives me each of her feet on the second request and is well-nigh impossible to catch if my truck is already hooked to the trailer, knowing from first light when I walk out with plans to ride her in lessons.

She seemingly lives to provoke me, relishing the thought of a fight. I am learning to choose my battles.

I have: worked her more, worked her less, over-and-undered her, sweet talked her, ignored her, bribed her, changed tactics, held the course. She, to her credit, remains who she is. I have sold her when I thought she was ready and then, humbled, hauled her home again. I have trusted her during long, hard days as well as stepped her out of line for red ribbons.

Always, I sit tight and keep smiling, knowing full well that Doll was, is and always will be, more or less in charge.

Like I said, it's not easy getting people to take a chance on you, whether you're a strong-willed mare or a middle-aged woman. As to our entwined destinies, I make no predictions. She is not a credit to my program, yet I am proud of her. Like her mistress, Doll is resolved to keeping her high-end baggage, preferring to be asked nicely rather than told.

If you're looking to buy a horse, don't buy one that is in a daily program if you, at best, ride only a few times each month. If you primarily trail ride, don't shop in the arenas. It isn't fair to you; it isn't fair to the horse.

If you're a rider who needs a great deal of control, don't buy the horse who revels in freedom of movement, the one who can — and must — go for miles. If you're a rider who follows a strict 'snaffles only' program, don't buy the finished bridle horse who has worked years to pack iron. Why not? I'll repeat, it isn't fair to the horse.

Riders, we need to get honest with where we're at in the saddle. Reluctance to do so is the biggest reason it's hard to find a horse/rider match. If you're afraid, even just a little bit, then own it. If you no longer ride as often or as athletically as you did a few years ago, then say so. If your riding interests have changed direction, then go with it. As horsemen, we've all been there; we're not going to judge.

Yessiree, we've got ourselves a situation.

The little voice I don't like listening to has been trying to get my attention these last few weeks, ever since I had an oops! moment with Tom Jones. It happened while things were going well, while we were having fun and it had nothing to do with the pony himself. I'd harnessed him carelessly and had come close to causing a wreck. I wrote about this a month or so ago and I honestly thought it was over and forgotten. I was wrong.

The upshot of the whole thing is that while I figuratively smacked my forehead and shrugged it off, the pony wasn't able to. He — the poster boy for learning how to drive, going from a zero to a hero — has lost his confidence.

This happens sometimes with the ones who have found everything easy; they'll hit that first bump in the road and the wheels fall off. I know Tom's rattled because he's always been bright eyed and bushy tailed, wanting to visit, chumming around and 'helping' me with chores.

No longer. The little gelding is evasive, wanting to fly under my radar and has even grown hard to catch. One contributing factor was a change in the weather shortly after our incident. It turned into a two-week cold snap and the pony was turned out. You know, if we turn them out when they're going well, they'll come back better. If we turn them out when they're going through a rough patch, they'll be downright complicated when we next cross paths. So it has proven with Tom.

Unfortunately, little about training — horses in general and driving horses in particular — is a smooth and gradual ascent. We can tip-toe around a hole that's there and pretend it's not but that's dangerous thinking. Frankly, it's the root of too many wrecks.

Instead, it's my job to go back as far as we need to, to find the place where the pony feels good. It will be before his time in the cart, before his time on the harrows and the stoneboat. Maybe even back to his days of long-lining, or working on the lunge. Rebuilding his confidence, convincing him that he is still worthy, that he is not junk.

I am wishing I still had my old driving pony, who, if paired with Tom, would far better teach these things that somehow I have not.

Small ponies, I find, believe all too often that they are disposable garbage. Too many have been taught this all their lives. The biggest thing with turning them around and getting them to a good place, is in getting them to change their minds about themselves. I'm sad that I put Tom among these shadows. Now, it's time to go find the light.

When you haul your new horse or pony home, try keeping change to a minimum. Remember, you liked him well enough to buy him in the first place. There might be a period of adjustment while he grows accustomed to his new environment — and even your care and expectations might seem strange. This adjustment period can range from mere days to many months and guess what? The level to which he is trained has little bearing on whether or not he'll be homesick.

If the seller recommends a particular bit or teacher or feed to try, why not go along with it, at least until your partnership starts to gel? Then, gradually, you can work towards change. This empathetic approach mightn't be the quickest one — but ultimately, it will help your horse step confidently into his new life.

This thing we do that has us not wanting to admit we're scared has got to stop. I'm fairly handy —and I'm frightened to get on certain horses. I am.

If I know there's a probability of one hurting me, once that thought is out there, guess what? Given the right time and the right place, he will. Experience has proven this, over 'n' over again — and yet we'll arm ourselves with online fear management courses or deep breathing exercises or horse cookies — and what's worse, we get used to riding afraid. So, what the heck are we ashamed of?

We'll freely admit we're scared of an icy road or an intimidating man. Why is it so darned hard to say we're scared of a twelve-hundred-pound horse with less than honourable intentions?

It's time to open a conversation, if not with everyone else, then at least with ourselves. I realize that the current horse culture wants us to believe there are bad people, but no bad horses. That if we just read 'em right, we'll get by.

Well, I'm gonna tell you that some horses are counterfeit sons o' bitches; they'll find your hole and that's all there is to it. Doesn't matter whether they were born dishonest, or if somebody made 'em that way. Doesn't matter who is to blame. If they scare us, they don't belong with us. I will always believe that it's a healthy thing, keeping only the honest, kindest horses and people around me. It is not failure, sending all others away.

Remember, we have choices. We can get hurt or we can get real. Fearing for our safety should never be tied to shame.

Horses can have deep-seated fears. I'm riding a new gelding that's really freaked out by boggy ground. Good thing he lives in bone dry southern Alberta. Seriously, though, it's an annoyance and it's not safe when he decides to take the plunge and gets to thrashing around.

I'm back at the beginning, wanting this fellow to trust me about where I ask him to put his feet. After 'sending' from the ground, over poles, tarps and horror of horrors, little puddles and mud — we're ready to ride — yet I can still feel his genuine terror over stepping into two or three inches of dirty water. Without undue pressure, I keep his nose to the puddle and when he's ready, he has all the rein he needs to stretch down and check it out.

A horse sniffing the ground will seldom jump but tends to step carefully when he's good and ready. It's a win-win as I work on my patience and he works on his trust. Before long, we've navigated every wet pothole down the laneway and soon, we'll be ready to ford the creek.

As an aside, I keep 'forgetting' to turn off the water at the trough. It's a lazy man's training but every little bit helps. I think it's working. Today, Charlie was 'puddle jumping', dining off all the tender shoots that grow along the spring below the yard. He was sheer mud to the elbows but I cheered for him in his victory.

"I hear you're not riding any more, that Mike is doing it all. Why'd you stop?" asked a friend that I was lunching with in town. I made some sort of sassy reply but on the long drive westward, had to admit that her comment really got to me. Why? Did it hit too close to home? Or did it bother me that someone thinks I'm all talk and no action?

I take a huge amount of ownership in the fact that I do this thing, aka Keystone, on my own initiative. I buy the horses, train them, wreck — and fix — all my own equipment, solve problems, reach out to prospective clients through my words, then sell the finished products like a grownup. All on my little lonesome. Or do I?

This past week has seen me run into a training issue that required Mike's help, both in the physical sense and in moral support. I was afraid that I was going to bite off more than I could chew. Let me be clearer: I was afraid. My long-suffering partner observed me quietly but he emboldened me enough to go 'n' get 'er done. You see, when you work alone, you're inclined to play it safe. I call it stayin' alive.

Later on, I begged him to do Doll's feet. This is something I should either be doing myself, or paying a farrier to do but he helped me, anyway.

I guess what I'm having to explore here is that we are not our own islands. We may fight and claw our way to some state of autonomy but if we're lucky, there are people around us who want us to do better and be our very best. They need not be a huge herd but just a few safe, trustworthy folks to become our tribe.

When we can't be our own heroes, they have our backs, be they in boots and spurs or in capes.

Doctoring.

Is there anything more demoralizing than going out to the gang and finding a cut or a kick? Again?

While I feel for you, I really do, just know that doctoring an injury can be a blessing in disguise. No horse likes the washing of cuts or getting needles but the handling — the plain, old-fashioned tender, loving care — can be the making of your relationship. Often, we've started out treating a young or dodgy pony who's touchy around the legs and feet and by the time we're back in the saddle, he's plumb gentle.

Follow the rules: stay safe; get veterinary advice (code for no motor oil or turpentine, for heaven's sake — if you wouldn't put it on your own cuts, then don't use it on your horse); if you think it needs stitching, get it stitched, and don't pick at stuff, if you can help it. Be gentle. Work quietly. Wonders can be wrought with cool, running water or 'Tea for Ten' — a ten-minute soak in a pail of warm Red Rose tea.

Happy Father's Day to all you men who make a difference. This day is a bittersweet one for our family, as the man who was Dad to us is now gone. Feeling nostalgic, I made sure to stop and appreciate the piece of old folk art, a rendition of 'End of the Trail' that he'd whittled from a cedar fence post a long, long time ago.

For better or worse, my Dad is probably the one who most modelled who I am. Athletic, personable, horse crazy, artistic, musical, also temperamental, impatient and maybe prone to such unmentionables as addiction and depression. He was so supportive of my riding. Until my dying day, I will remember waiting in those line ups, searching the stands for either his thumbs up or his commiserative smile and shrug. It was a wonderful thing, watching him do the same for his grandkids.

I love you Dad. It wasn't always an easy trail but I sure wish it had been longer.

It's a misconception that I'm a fearless old bird, willing to climb on anything that strikes my fancy. Not so. Life has a way of taking the wind out of our sails and the reasons aren't always what we might imagine.

A fear of riding can stem from long periods of time away from the saddle … to becoming a mother … to watching a child or friend get hurt … to having survived serious illness. Heck, we don't even have to have been bucked off or run away with.

In my case, after an unremarkable lifetime in the saddle, coming through it more or less unscathed, I had a stroke in my early forties. I survived, which was good, but I was droolly, tottery and depressed ... and I was left very, very shaken. My counsellor eventually urged me to throw caution to the wind and get back to my horses.

I was miserable without riding but I'd not set foot in a stirrup for close to three years and I was surprised to find that I was scared to do so. What if I had another stroke, or had my brain ooze out my ear, or... my imagination provided no shortage of gory endings.

And so, I started. Riding a good and decent horse, paying a trusted professional to guide me, keeping the demands low by joining a basic horsemanship group. My habit of holing up in hushed and darkened rooms had left me unfit and dizzy, impaired hearing left me struggling to keep up to the rest of the class, fine motor skills and the ability to concentrate were pretty darned shaky. I hadn't even been driving, let alone hauling my trailer down the highway ... but I got 'er done.

Growing a little stronger week by week, gaining mere grains of confidence in my ability to remember certain things and forget others. I persevered. That was eleven years ago and nowadays, I can't give thanks enough for how it's shaken out.

If you've lost confidence, even if you don't know why, take heart. You CAN build it up again. You might need a new teacher, a different riding environment, most likely a safer horse. But if you loved riding once upon a time, you can learn to love it all over again. I promise.

Many of us have withstood so much in the name of getting good at getting by. I'll go so far as to say that, judging from some of the notes sent me, you've seen your fair share of abuse. "Cowboy up!" "Show him who's boss!" "Get right back up there!" "Don't show him you're afraid!" I could go on but won't; I reckon you've heard them all.

You've sent me stories of absolute heroics. "I knew he was badly hurt and that it was up to me to get his foot out of the stirrup and call the ambulance." "Something happened to me when I became a single mom and everything was my responsibility. I knew I could not get hurt." "I had so much trust in my old horse but I've never found another one to replace her." "I gained a fair bit of weight and found out the hard way that my new body didn't work like my old one did." "I used to ride like the wind and now I play wreck after imaginary wreck in my head." "I'm incontinent and between being prepared for emergencies and remembering to pee before I ride, I just feel like a ticking time-bomb."

"At our stable, everyone's jumping and while I used to, I was always nervous. I was assigned the horses that weren't super safe and little by little, it chipped at my courage." "I come from an amazing horse family but something was always wrong with me …" "I watched my daughter get badly hurt one ordinary, happy day." "I wish I didn't feel like a failure for being afraid to ride but I lie awake at night with it. Riding is all I've ever wanted to do." "Against my wishes, I was talked into buying a horse I had no business owning." "Arthritis and ageing have taken their toll." You get the drift …

Many of you wrote to me in tears, saying this was the first you'd put such thoughts into words, feelings of which even your family and friends knew nothing. Some of your stories were very hard for me, there was so much pain in them. I've read them all and I thank you for sharing. Know that you are not alone; your story is echoed in the stories of many others.

I believe that this very act of writing will lighten your burden and make way for something good to take its place. Burying fear and past trauma, hoping it will die within hasn't helped many of us. There is much healing to be had in sharing. Meanwhile, I'm going to say it again: fear is our wisdom, keeping us safe.

Victory comes in many ways. Today, it came quietly, in the form of one small pony, just doing a job that he's become way too worried about.

Tom had a great few months in harness, learning to harrow my pens and arena, eventually working happily and confidently in the cart. All this, until one day when we had a harness malfunction and I was forced to run the panicked pony into a wire fence to get stopped. While it could've been far worse, the pony lost all his sparkle.

We've been made to backtrack, to white knuckle our way through things that were once a breeze. So today, another day putting the pony on the stone boat, another day with him wild eyed, tension turning his bowels to water ...

Then, a change. Tom put his head down, began to breathe and just walked it out. It's only a little old pony, some might say. To me, though, helping Tom Jones through this is something that matters a lot.

You're only as cool as your horse is.

This hard fact of life is hitting home today, as we prepare for another branding. After years of riding awesome cow horses with high mileage in the school of hard knocks, I'm contemplating which of my youngsters I'll shepherd through today's gathering. There will be no sorting in the gate, no awesome moves on slippery hillsides, no heroic efforts in the actual branding pen. But we have to start somewhere.

If you're one of the folks on an old standby, I urge you, salute him and give him your best. Be appreciative. Riding the perfect ranch horse is a state of grace that doesn't last forever. It's another lesson learned.

BLESSINGS

Living near running water is good feng shui. It's good for your horses, it's good for your soul. We regularly use a fifteen-minute soak to cool the legs down after a strenuous day or a long trailer haul.

Did you know the same treatment, along with a brisk walk home to get the blood moving, is the old-time cure for grass founder? This runs in the face of modern science, but I stand by decades of personal experience. You will have a few bad days on the regimen of creek soaks and hand walking. But it works.

Keep the soakings short but do as many of them per day as you possibly can, followed by a brisk walk or trot as the patient is able. A soak in the creek always works wonders on wire cuts, puffy legs, hot spots, lameness and even malaise from overtraining or depression. It's a chance to bond with your horse quietly, playfully, with tender loving care. Soaking teaches her to trust you and to love water, two good things in anyone's book.

If you live near running water, you are blessed.

If asked, most of us would say that having fun was why we got involved with horses in the first place. If riding is no longer fun for you, I'm sorry. Please take time to reflect and really find out why. Whatever the reason — fear, guilt, boredom, health, frustration, burn out, money — are you ripe for a change?

I'll admit to feeling any of the above at different times throughout my life — and my riding has evolved because of it. A serious health scare, subsequent job loss, ageing, then watching friends and family members get hurt with horses have all taken their toll. I've accepted that certain horse sports and certain types of horses will never be a comfortable fit for me and that's okay.

A day spent in friendship and camaraderie, bringing on one of my young horses, still makes my heart soar. No, it's definitely not the Olympics — but maybe it's close enough.

We all admire the beautiful mover. You know, the horse that stops the breath, the one that steals the longing gaze of every eye upon him, the horse that people wish was their own. Thing is, we can all be riding a better mover than the one we currently have. Yes, you read that right. The following is a list of working techniques that can open up a whole new world to how your horse moves at any gait, whether you sit in English or Western tack.

Do the chiro and bodywork; a sore horse is a stiff horse. Fit your saddle to the individual animal; like shoes, saddles are not one size fits all. Put the saddle in the correct place behind the shoulder; a saddle too far ahead kills the stride. See to the teeth. Make sure your horse is fed correctly, neither kept too fat, or just as bad, too thin. Give him plenty of turnout time.

Teach your horse or pony to stretch. Alternating your riding time between minutes of stretching downwards from nose to tail with minutes of riding roundly on a soft, soft feel will strengthen and lengthen his carrying muscles without shortening him. Once he can do so, he will truly relax. Do not be miserly in your approach; learn how to give.

Insist that your horse walk and trot within his capabilities. That means that he must be encouraged to use himself beyond a lazy shuffle, as small movement shrinks elasticity. Free paces work on the horse much like a yoga class. This forwardness is not the same thing as making the horse rush around, however, because that will destroy his natural swing.

Every horse has an inborn rhythm; our job as his teacher is to find it and allow it to grow and become his default. In order to find this rhythm, we must sustain the gait long enough for the horse to relax, drop his guard and enjoy the full play of his muscles. When we do many transitions and changes of direction, he is unable to soften and maintain forwardness. Large curves and gentle changes of bend in big "S" shapes are the kindest ways to do this. Encourage the big trot by slowly but energetically opening the back of the knee while posting. Doing this will activate the horse's hind end.

Transitions are vital tools and a meter of our training progress but they are not the way to initially teach our horse to move well. Done too often, they will cause a horse to worry and become mentally and physically tired, states that do not encourage the swing and joyfulness that are hallmarks of good movement. No transition is ever better than the gait preceding it. Improve the rhythm and relaxation of the basic gaits, first.

Riding out as much as possible will develop your horse's enjoyment in how he moves. If he is not comfortable riding out of the arena, this should be developed gradually until he is at home in the great outdoors. The sunshine, the uneven terrain, the joy of 'going someplace real'… all are key in bringing any horse to the height of his natural beauty.

Make occasional use of trot poles, spaced correctly for your horse's stride. Shorten your stirrups. Develop your position so that you can get out of the saddle and free up his back to lift and swing. Memorize this feeling, as it is your guiding light. Trotting through shallow water such as puddles, tall grass or snow will have the same benefit.

Smile while riding, look up, lighten up, have fun. Our goal as horsemen is to develop the horse to the point where he improves with our training, where he gets stronger, healthier and happier the farther along he is in his schooling, even as he reaches old age. When we consider how few working horses can claim this achievement, surely it behooves us to try.

Good horsemen know that the day is made better when everyone knows their job. So often, buyers tell us they "don't need a schooled show horse, they just want to ride". Yes, well, that's a bit like playing the piano with two fingers, when real music can bring so much joy.

Whether you're working cows all day or riding the trails, the way is made smoother with a horse or pony with power brakes, power steering and cruise control, one who keeps his shoulders up on the turns, gives a soft feel and happily, calmly takes direction. A worthwhile goal is to keep your horse slowly, steadily improving and 'on the same page'. Remember, good horsemen take pride in their ride!

With so many mares, their goodness is their gift to us. It is not given lightly and should never be taken for granted. To do so means that bit by bit, they will rescind their trust and kindness — two things, I have found, very difficult to put back. The hard mares, the ones we call troubled, have so often been handled by hurting or damaged people. Yes, we need to think about that.

Geldings seem especially able to absorb our issues, hence their popularity. Mares, on the other hand, can be like holding up mirrors.

Each of us does one thing better than anyone else out there. It might be an ability to put a lovely finish on a horse ... or communicate with clients ... or start colts ... or understand problem horses ... or write great ads ... or instill confidence in timid riders ... but we all have that one thing.

For years, I was ashamed of my inability to stay focused in just one area of the horse world. As soon as things got too expensive or too serious, I'd be moving on, to be eclipsed by others who'd stay in that particular discipline. Eventually, I realized that in my line of discovering raw talent, recognizing where certain horses might best fit, my wide-spread experience was a positive attribute.

Nowadays, it's easy for me to work a horse or pony and early on, see where it might sparkle and shine. I'll scan a group of beasts swishing flies in the pasture and if one sets me a-tingle, I know he'll make a champion. I don't know if this makes me a dreamer or an eternal optimist but I think of it as a gift.

These skills will never get me to the winner's circle because I haven't the single-minded determination to make it happen. But if that's where you long to be, I might be able to help you.

I hadn't seen him for nine or ten years. Both of us moving a little slower, perhaps broader through the beam, he said he still knew me. I called his name and his head swung 'round in a long, knowing look. Who could blame me for tearing up, just a little, when he turned from his mates and walked over, touching my arm, blowing softly in my face.

To most people, he's just an old pony. To me, he's a lion heart who never, ever, let me down. After it was all over between us and he had moved on, I was window shopping one day, when a silver bracelet made of snaffle bits and a lone heart charm engraved with the word 'Magic' caught my eye. Serendipity. It recalled a gentleman I'd grown to love, even though he'd never be mine. Black Magic, thank you. It was an honour to have held your reins.

If we're not careful, this horse thing we do can obliterate all the reasons we love them in the first place. The pressure before the shows, the looming sales try outs, the gut-wrenching regularity of board and vet bills ...

If we are willing, we can stop and reset ourselves to what really matters. Even if they are our livelihood, when horses are in our blood, we need the feel and the smell of them ... the sound of a happy snort, the morning whinny, the softening of an eye when we smooth a forelock, the beautiful energy of contented munching after we've thrown the hay.

Yesterday, my grown daughter and I shared the rare gift of a ride to the creek. She lives far away and we don't have many of these any more. Unpacking an impromptu picnic, letting the ponies soak and graze while we settled on an old log, it was amusing to watch their personalities come alive as we drifted away from routine. Doll, shyly showing her playful side in the water, then inquiring of the nuts I'd brought. Parry, bolder, begging for a taste of garlic sausage! Sun-kissed faces relaxed into smiles as we reminisced about these characters and their little foibles — a reminder that to know an animal such as a horse or a dog, is not a right but a blessing.

Then, riding bareback, made lazy with the heat and the sound of running water, we reined our ponies up the hills to make the long way home.

Horsemanship is a fine balance. We get stuck on obedience and responsiveness, then find our pony is too reactive and tense. Or we work at relaxing our partnership, then find our boundaries and leadership have gone out the window. Why is this and what can we do?

To start, everything we do when handling our horses either livens them up or it desensitizes them. Examples of livening exercises would be round penning with quick changes in direction, or riding turnarounds or halt-to-canter (or trot) transitions. Hot, 'go-go' horses find these things a walk in the park. In fact, if you overdo them, you'll end up with a chargey ride.

The flip side has us doing our bombproofing exercises, such as sacking out with a slicker or working with a flag. Heck, even a few kids playing in the arena will do the job. Quiet, gentle horses are often overly desensitized and they become dull, swishy, even cranky. We see these ones and think they're 'dead to the world'. Riders who kick regularly while they ride, or nag their horses with repetitious cues, are surprised to find they are desensitizing their animals like the dude string on a trail ride. Ironically, ponies with 'baggage' or prior abuse are often extremely spooky and they require really active bombproofing. When we try to handle them with tact and kid gloves, they usually get worse.

I'm not a huge fan of timed cowboy challenge competitions, necessarily, but I like how a little work in this direction can make our horse unafraid of umbrellas, bicycles or jackets going on and off. Sound proofing, such as clanking metal or running hoof beats, is essential in training a safe driving pony. Likewise, crowd noises and PA sounds are excellent in schooling any horse destined for competition. One of our very best show horses began turning crowd noise into a full-blown phobia. We successfully treated her with a looped party recording of Oktoberfest!

The trick, of course, is in finding the balance point between gentling and livening on a regular basis. This becomes even more challenging because each pony and horse in our care requires a different mix to achieve his best. What wins with one, often doesn't make inroads with another. Find that balance and the partnership will become one of trust and willing cooperation.

The good news? Once you start thinking about this, it will come quicker than you imagine.

One of the problems about riding out in spring, ironically, is what makes it wonderful. Namely, we've often spent the winter going 'round and 'round indoors. Suddenly, we've 'green grass fever' with super-nutritious food and all living things from mighty trees to little ponies can feel their sap a-rising.

It is no accident that most horse wrecks happen this time of year. Horses and ponies, either unridden for six months or else used to the monotony of the darkened arena, come to life when the wind whispers things in their ears. Spring grass, even in slight amounts, is so full of energy that the happy grazers are bustin' out all over. Worse, hormonal cycles in our mares are at their absolute strongest this time of year. In combination, all these things can challenge our horsemanship.

So, what to do? Be patient — this, too, shall pass — and be proactive. Ride lots. If our horses aren't sweating on the neck, shoulders and flanks when you're finished, you didn't work them hard enough. Prolonged outdoor workouts using second and third gears (without short bursts of excitement like galloping and jumping) for the first little while will keep fresh ponies focused. Do some groundwork, especially lungeing at canter, for ten or fifteen minutes before anyone steps aboard. Control the amount of grazing time, which is essential for most ponies anyway, throughout the whole of the summer. And be careful with the moods of mares during May and June; give them lots of exercise because they need the movement — a dose of Bute for back pain if necessary — and talk to your vet about hormone therapy, like Regumate, if your 'good time gal' has morphed into a monster.

Riding outside is good medicine. It puts the spring in the step, the joy in the day. It is the celebration of surviving another winter. Just be aware of these game changers — and take heart in the knowledge that by late summer, we'll be working as hard as our horses are, just getting a forward step.

Dressage training? Head for the hills.

At a driving event many years ago, the head official asked the name of my dressage teacher during the awards banquet. He'd been impressed by the lowering of my pony's haunches during the lengthenings in our test. All I could tell him was that beyond the long-ago tutelage of the inimitable E.M. Boerschmann, my dressage learning had been a long and lonely road. Literally. In fact, I was too ashamed to tell him where I'd really figured out what was going on.

As a kid training my driving pony, Sovereign, I'd noticed that his loin would coil and the musculature change while climbing hills, the same as it did the very few times he'd properly extended his trot. Aha! I learned to train for the lengthened trot on gentle inclines. Sovy quickly learned the required response when I'd ask for this in the show ring — no small feat for a pony who naturally moved like a runaway sewing machine.

Even now, I train for lengthenings and upward transitions on gentle inclines. I ask for shortenings, downward transitions and reinback, (if the horse is experienced and the carriage not too heavy) while pointed slightly downhill. Driving or riding, it's equally effective. To this day, I see a bit of a slope and immediately commence a few circles. I get the results I'm looking for, without quickening the paces, hollowing the back, stressing the pony ... all the usual blood, sweat and tears.

It can be hard keeping all those horse training gurus and their mantras straight — the secrets and keys to success in the saddle, when to back off, when to press on. I thought so, too, until a brilliant teacher explained it all very well to me. "First, teach your horse to happily go forward, turn left, turn right, stop and back up." He may have been joking but a lifetime later, his advice is still good.

There's just something about horses. Those of us who are spiritually and emotionally plugged into them remember an ancient knowledge that we seem born with. It defies all reckoning.

My mother recalls moments when I was very young. I'd come in from the barn and tell her what the horses were thinking. In one case, I knew one was about to get sick. The pony grew ill, of course, and I don't know how or why I knew, I just did. Every so often I'll come across another such child and I'm struck by how much ancient wisdom surrounds him, or her, despite tender years on this earth.

Perhaps this explains why we 'kids who love horses' never quite seem to outgrow it, no matter how relentless the pressure of growing up. Moving to the city or ageing into the old folks' home is surely no cure. The energy of an unrequited horse person is so beautiful, sad and fierce.

More powerful than anything, this connection that some of us have with horses feels as vital as blood and oxygen. I still lie awake nights, wondering, wondering. What is it all for?

NOTES

NOTES

Flicka, the pony who started it all. Homely by any standards, her honesty and reliability will always render her beautiful to my eyes.

AUTHOR'S COLLECTION

Gypsy was the first pony I'd trained, start to finish. Could anything be worse than to be taught by an eight-year-old kid?

AUTHOR'S COLLECTION

By age eight, I'd begun riding sidesaddle. This picture, on the beautiful Peter, was taken before a School Pony class at the fair. I was dressed as the teacher, in my great-grandmother's cape.

AUTHOR'S COLLECTION

Eclipse. The equine love of my life, an off-track Thoroughbred that I trained and competed under the tutelage of Mrs. Boerschmann. These were hard and lonely years, but I found out how much I loved and needed horses.

AUTHOR'S COLLECTION

Plans to continue riding in Germany were shelved when I met, and then married, Mike. Silk top hats and square halts were replaced with Stetsons and chasing cows.

AUTHOR'S COLLECTION

Like many ranching families, we spent weekdays in the saddle, and hauled horses to show on weekends. The kids tagged along. It was a time that predates modern safety.

AUTHOR'S COLLECTION

I spent a lot of time holding the lines of these two fire-breathing dragons. Kinistino and Kananaskis were outstanding Welsh mares owned by my mother-in-law; the bobsleigh and harness belonged to my dad.

AUTHOR'S COLLECTION

The Family Class, seldom seen anymore, required us to walk, jog and lope in formation. Like playing 'crack the whip', woe betide those unfortunates who were stuck on the ends.

AUTHOR'S COLLECTION

'Til my dying day, I will remember this pony, Kinistino, waltzing around the yard, to the sound of laughing children and barking dogs. Iain and Caitlin, aged eight and six, made many such miles with Rowan, our Sheltie.

AUTHOR'S COLLECTION

On the top of the world, with Annie, at calving time. Riding out in the real world helped our ponies' show careers, while learning the skills for showing made them better on the ranch ... thus was born the 'rule of fifty-fifty'.

AUTHOR'S COLLECTION

In eighteen years of carriage driving competition, Highland Piper was beaten once. The day I retired Piper's show harness, cleaned it and hung it on the highest hook, it came as no surprise that he had just passed on.

AUTHOR'S COLLECTION

The creek is as much a part of Keystone as am I. The horses and ponies all love it here, playing, splashing and soaking away their troubles.

AUTHOR'S COLLECTION

Cody got me back in the game when I feared it was over. A good horse puts back what misfortune has taken away.

NOAH FALLIS PHOTOGRAPHY

Winning isn't everything. Being safe, competent and confident is where the joy lies. When these are established, the winning can take care of itself!

AUTHOR'S COLLECTION

On Ritz, flag bearing at the Guy Weadick Pro Rodeo in High River, Alberta. In 1912, Guy Weadick masterminded the first ever Calgary Stampede.

TWISTED TREE PHOTOGRAPHY

Summer 2005 was a season of unimaginable highs and lows. I was strangely, profoundly unwell. Doctors merely laughed. Winning the Battle of the Breeds at Spruce Meadows with Team Welsh and Black Magic was a welcome diversion.

AUTHOR'S COLLECTION

Romance on the range! But wait, all is not as it seems. Mike has been entrusted with the day's allotment of trail mix in his coat pocket, and by lunch time, it is gone. Mid-scolding, I am silenced with a kiss.

AUTHOR'S COLLECTION

Two weeks after winning this sidesaddle race on Cisco, I had a stroke. I was forty-two, housebound, out of work, and forbidden by my doctor to ride. Depression loomed. For better or worse, I was starting to find out who I really was.

AUTHOR'S COLLECTION

My healing began when a counsellor said, "Do what you loved when you were a kid." And so, I began. Terrified, shaking, I signed up with a good teacher. Week by week, I grew a little braver, stronger, more like me.

AUTHOR'S COLLECTION

We all need someone who will cheer us on. As I healed, Mike gave me the courage to start riding as a full-time career.

NOAH FALLIS PHOTOGRAPHY

This is the first sidesaddle I built on the custom Rod Nikkel tree. It was a proud moment to ride, and then race, on this rig after so many hours spent on its cutting-edge design.

AUTHOR'S COLLECTION

There is something about the flowing apron, the serene rider and the cantering horse that fires imagination. Here, Henry and I lope into the centrefold of the AQHA publication, America's Horse.

AUTHOR'S COLLECTION

In 2018, I was honoured to be among the first eight women to race, sidesaddle, in front of the iconic Stampede Grandstand. Oh, the sheer wall of noise from 45,000 screaming rodeo fans, as we rounded that final turn!

LORRAINE HJALTE PHOTOGRAPHY

In 2019, I joined the legendary voice of rodeo, Mr. Bob Tallman, to announce the ladies' sidesaddle races at the Calgary Stampede. What a thrill!

AUTHOR'S COLLECTION

SUMMER
Learning

Summer is about abundance ... about learning more. When we approach our experience, our competition and our horsemanship from an educational standpoint, there is no winning or losing, no room for comparisons or failings. Everything we do with our horses becomes what is needed to create the whole.

As we age, we become more aware of the beauty in the ordinary. The days of summer will be what we remember when we look back on it all. We know this and promise ourselves that if nothing else, we will not waste them. We will be more aware ...

For many of us, summer is also a time of showing. I wish you well but I also wish you mindfulness. Know when that little voice inside is leading you astray ... putting too much pressure on ... forgetting to do what is right for your horse, or your child ... smothering the reason you fell in love with horses in the first place. We are tested sorely when we put it all on the line for victory! Too often, while we're achieving good things in competition, we're also feeling the greatest shame in our horsemanship.

This is when I must focus on bettering myself, on the purity found in my schooling. I think about quality time. What do I need to change in order to make my horse happier and healthier than he was at the beginning of the year? Sometimes, I need to change nothing. Most times, though, I need to adjust my ego and my innate need to win. I get back to loving my horse. I stop trying to be right. I strive to learn to do better.

When this happens, I am usually rewarded with internal peace and often, with outward success, as well. Good news is, if the first is present, the second is no longer key to my happiness.

IT'S A GOOD LIFE ...
IF YOU DON'T WEAKEN

Happy Canada Day! As is usual, Mike and I spent the day in the saddle, being among the public and allowing so many children an opportunity to pet a real, live horse. Well, that was the plan. Reality took a sharp turn when I was given a humbling lesson. My horse isn't as broke as I'd thought.

I think from her point of view, any one or two of these things would have been doable: the military band, the marksmanship, the hundreds of tiny children running around waving flags, the surging crowd wanting to pet her, the buffalo, pigs and chickens, the umbrellas and baby strollers, the tractors, the whip cracking exhibition, the live country music, the distant and unnaturally-still fibreglass bull, the thunderstorm rolling in from the west... and me sidesaddle.

What proved to be her final unhingeing, however, was the Percheron team pulling the large covered wagon over the bridge. Suddenly, with a real flair for the dramatic, she told me we were about to check out of Dodge.

At one point, during our airs above the ground, my ruminations as to whether the one hundred and thirty-year-old saddle was going to hold together were interrupted by a lovely lady approaching from the side. "Are you Keystone?" she asked. "I love following you and I always read your page!" Oh, great, I can remember thinking, wouldn't you know it? I was unable to grasp her hand and stop to chat because I, a grown woman, couldn't handle my pony. It was a situation that would have been comical if it hadn't been so bloody awful. During the national anthem, we actually withdrew from the ceremony, as we were causing a decidedly un-Canadian stir.

Alone at the trailer, I was ready to load up, go home and drink beer in the hammock. Except there was something basic but monumental to sort out here. I carefully took off the old silver bridle, the romal reins, the treasured sidesaddle ... and geared up with a colt bridle and my workaday rig. Now she wouldn't have me over a barrel with my precious things.

I slipped her cavesson and lunge rein on, cinched up and went off to a private corner.

Soon, her mind came back to me, her head dropped and she started swinging 'round at an easy lope. Then the licking and chewing, the sneezing, the slowed tempo all told me that she was ready to try again. And so we did. Relaxed, happy and smiling, we rode among the crowd in celebration of this country that we love.

Winston Churchill wrote that he liked the idea of learning, he just hated the being taught. Today, I learned a lesson — that you're only as cool as your horse is. God only knows where I left my ego. I haven't seen it since ten o'clock.

The old-timers called it a 'sick' wind, that on-edge keening that keeps chipping away at you from the south-east. It puts horses out of their minds, cattle on the fight — and farm wives thinking of greener pastures.

Today's wind makes staying inside — paying bills, doing laundry, all the relentless, endless stuff — seem like a blessed relief. Then, happiness, when I find some folding money in the pocket of my old jeans!

On these hard days, the good stuff is still around us, we just have to notice it's there.

Here's something fun. I came upon the 1879 classic, Mrs. Beeton's Housewives' Treasury and a chapter called 'Riding, Driving and Boating'.

"Every lady who rides should understand the construction and fastenings of her horse's equipment and be able, in case of necessity, to do for herself. When there are men at hand, make them useful, but be able to do without...."

We've come a long way, baby.

We all have those days. Bills piling up. Kids having trouble. A cross word with our partner. The incessant, bloody wind. A lack of wellness, even soreness or depression. Heavy traffic and a stressful haul. Looming deadlines with upcoming shows. We all have 'em.

It's very easy to take this out on our horses.

A recent afternoon at the public arena shed some light on this. I watched people screeching in to the parking lot, jerking on their horses while they got ready to ride, really putting the pressure on between their hands and spurs, not taking time to warm up or reward the honest tries. Never letting up, not admitting to themselves that they were feeling fragile and needed to take care. Let's be honest, there are days we maybe shouldn't be riding.

Many of us were raised to turn our backs on our problems; to give no notice to weakness or churning emotions and to soldier on. This is how we got by. The problem with this 'get to work, you'll get better' mentality is that it can turn one into a human doing, as opposed to a human being. Compassion and empathy get tossed right out the door. We become dominators, just looking for the next big fight.

For me, a long timer in this band of brothers, recognizing when I'm in the mood to ride mad and laying it out there is key. "Hey, dear horse, I'm really frail today. I'll need your help and a blessing just to ride with kindness." Then, I remind myself to breathe deeply and soften my face into a smile.

Most times, this is enough. It shifts me towards being happy, rather than being right.

In a world ruled by competition, nobody seems to haul to parades any more. We still consider them a gold mine of good training for an all 'round saddle horse, making a point of taking ours to whatever local festivities we can find. If they hold it together amongst the marching bands, bagpipes, floats, painted curbs, manhole covers and balloons, they'll find the average show a walk in the park.

There's a lot we can do to make parade day enjoyable, even for an inexperienced horse. First, we want to make sure he's broke, that he understands the word whoa and that waiting is the most important speed. Perhaps a little desensitization? Carrying a slicker, dragging a tire on the rope, perhaps walking over plywood or through puddles and at our house, standing at the hitching rail while we play Grandad's loudly crashing "Military Pipes and Drums at the Royal Tattoo".

By the time we've reached maximum volume without wigging out, we're pretty much ready to order a round of tankards and don our kilts.

Most importantly, we make sure that our new parade horse is accompanied by a bona fide mentor, a horse we know and trust to take pride in the job. This, alone, does much to give our fellow a positive first day out. Before too long, it's a matter of wavin', hootin' and hollerin', as the horses play to the crowd.

I have a crooked horse. (Yes, most of us do.) One of the goals of training is to slowly, gently, systematically straighten our animal's inherent crookedness. Heck, we're all born favouring either our right or left sides. But any ride on this green-broke mare, despite chiropractic work and mindful schooling, always has me bleeding inside the right knee. Today was no exception. When I dismounted after she'd settled well and had given me one hundred percent, a tell-tale patch of red was spreading across the denim of my jeans.

A wise, old vet once told me that when he was diagnosing lameness or soreness in riding horses, he always asked the owner where his, or her, own body hurt. I've always remembered this. Can a rider feel soreness in her own body, without it affecting her horse, in turn? Who really knows for sure? I've simply decided that if I start to hurt while I'm training, it's probably time to quit.

An aside, this was a diary entry from several years ago and it came as a surprise to read it again. Doll, who has been with me for four years now, has ceased to give me a sore knee for a very long time; she, herself, has softened and straightened to a marked degree. It is a reminder that our progress, while sometimes slow or subtle, is most often there. We need only to watch and wait.

On unreliability.

Despite popular thinking, it doesn't matter whether the problem began with bad handling, or whether there's a short in a pony's circuitry. It just doesn't matter. What does matter is whether you or I will knowingly send such a pony on into the world, or just as wrongly, insist that our children ride it.

We raised a splendid black pony, who genetically and environmentally, was made to be awesome. Some part of him, however, was programmed to kick, to double barrel anything that struck him oddly. Because he was young and beautiful, it seemed wrong to consider euthanasia. You can bet we did our darnedest to change him, including two winters spent feeding cows and choring on the bobsleigh.

Fast forward to an ordinary morning back in the barn. He and his partner had worked solidly for two hours, bedding down bulls. Then, in a flash while I removed his harness, he kicked out with lightning hooves, knocking the winter cap from my head.

It was the moment of reckoning. Way too close for comfort, I was incredibly fortunate. It was a harsh reminder that some personalities, man or beast, will never be worthy of our trust. Yes, another lesson learned.

Trialing a horse before purchase is a two-sided endeavour. Buyers are going to see if the real-life animal in any way resembles the horse that was advertised. Even if he's been well represented, liking a horse in pictures has no bearing on whether he will fit your personality, your program, or that indefinable magic called 'falling in love'.

There's a flip side to the trial ride and I'm finding it's one most buyers don't understand. As a seller, the trial ride is as much about whether I get a good feeling about my horse's future in your hands, as whether or not you want to own him. Going online is a boon when it comes to getting a feel for the sheer weight that horses have in a stranger's life. But try as I might, I sometimes underestimate a buyer's level of competency. I certainly have no way of guessing their confidence level or innate 'feel' when they ride.

I've been labelled a 'tire-kicker' when I didn't cut a check after a trial. I've also been accused of 'leading people on' when I've declined their purchase offer after seeing them ride. I know that long drives and flights are costly, that we all are busy — and based on prior communication, I may have honestly thought we could work out a deal.

In reality, the best thing I can do is go with my gut, knowing that as the seller, it's up to me to ensure my pony or horse will go on to a place where he will improve and thrive. If questioned, I will simply say my horse is not right for your job. It's not meant to be hurtful.

Here's the thing. Many of us are quick to talk a good game, to shy away from admitting we need more time in the saddle, or better instruction, or that we are afraid. Too many of us want Lamborghinis, when in reality, we would be better served with old Fords.

Like so many of you, I've been feeling anxious. My eyes scan the buckskin hills around us countless times each day. Do I smell more smoke than usual? Why are the cows bawling and so upset? Watching the news, my heart goes out to all the communities affected in the forested areas. So much gratitude is owed to the men and women who are fighting fire.

Those of us living in the grasslands are facing risks that are every bit as real. One lightning strike, one spark off a harvest machine, one tossed cigarette ... and we're just as vulnerable. The only way I know to lessen that anxiety, that three o'clock in the morning feeling, is to try and think ahead.

Emergency numbers and contacts of neighbours (including nearby Hutterite Colonies) are in all phones or in every vehicle, as are charged fire extinguishers, work gloves and heavy-duty wire cutters. Know your legal land description and write it down. Even in well-mowed areas, have a strict no idling policy.

Grass fires travel fast. Make sure that trucks are fueled up and water wagons are filled with sacks and shovels at the ready. Livestock trailers should be easy to get at and all the adults should know how to hook them up. Tack rooms can hold extra halters, water pails and a couple of small square bales of hay. Horses that you're planning to evacuate to safety must know how to be caught and get on the trailer when told.

Do a cleanup of the yard, including letting animals graze down the long grass in the farm yard that makes such quick, hot fuel. Make that overdue trip to the dump. As a fire preventative, make post piles and feed stacks at a distance from the buildings and in the opposite direction to the prevailing wind. We had to learn this one the hard way.

Have pet carriers and meds ready by the door. Make sure ID information is on each pet. Our horses can have tape 'collars' or tags braided into their manes with names and contact numbers in permanent marker. Not everyone will be able to do this if the livestock herds are large ones. In that case, you spray paint information on their backs as best you can and be ready to open gates and/or cut fences in strategic spots if there's a hurry to get out.

If an evacuation is necessary, think of all the emergency vehicles that will need access to your yard and property. Don't block access to the house or lock pasture gates. Turn off power and natural gas if you can, before you go. Know that rural property holders will be billed if the fire department comes to your aid, even if someone else has made the call. This is a small concern when things are blazing but make sure your insurance has coverage to help you out.

Monitor the local radio stations for news of evacuations and local safety protocols. Then, once we've done what little we can to be ready, we'll pray and hope like heck we don't need to try it out.

Mike and I are down to one personal horse, each. That's an all-time low for us but you know, they get more riding and attention this way. Without knowing just how it happens, we can own so many that feeding and husbandry take up all our time, energy and money. Simply put, nothing is left for the joy.

Be careful, though, because owning two horses can come at a cost. Buddying up, getting lonesome, being herdbound — whatever you call it — runs rife when horses are kept as a pair. Make a point of taking one or the other to town for lessons or public riding, in addition to riding alone at home because they have to be trained to be OK with separation. This is not only about going out alone, it's also about being left behind.

Everybody worries about 'the herdbound thing' but we need to realize that our horses worry about it, too. They need to be socialized — and this takes a plan consisting of knowledge, courage, a sense of timing and commitment. We've learned the hard way that herdboundness can change according to time of year, even with different riders on the same horse. Finally, while most horses can learn to handle separation, there is maybe a tiny percentage that cannot. If you're interested, tomorrow we'll talk.

"Help, my horse is herdbound!"

If I could name the biggest problem with owning horses, this would be it. Plainly put, a herdbound horse or pony is more interested in his friends than he is in you. It's an especially shadowy thing to nail down because the degree to which he acts out will often depend on who's riding him.

If you can imagine yourself back in high school for a minute, it will help you understand. Horses, like teenage girls, simply want to be in the group that makes them feel cool and tells them what to think and do. People love 'submissive' horses, thinking they will be easier to train but in our experience, the ones low in the herd pecking order are often desperate for leadership. These sweet and gentle horses can struggle the most with being alone, while their bossier herd mates are bravely striking out on their own. That said, we've found no correlation between breed, age, or sex and herdbound behaviour.

The method we use is non-confrontational and allows your horse to simply choose the behaviour and the consequence. It keeps the relationship friendly. While not requiring special skills as a bronc rider, it requires some forethought and often, setting the scene for success. Please note we do not use treats, as one cannot trade the core values of honour and respect for a cookie.

We'll start our ride by going to work right where he wants to be, right near his friends, riding vigorously at a hard trot with lots of tight directional changes, until both horse and rider have raised a good sweat. We don't try to fix herdboundness with loping, as so many horses get in a place where they stop learning and just get tough. Maybe in twenty minutes, maybe more, we'll quietly ride off a way. We'll just try him and see.

He'll either walk along sweetly, happy for the break, or he'll start acting up. If it's the first, praise him for his generosity with a loose rein walk and lots of petting; you'll soon be able to ask for more, by riding even farther away. If it's the second, which is more likely, ride him firmly back to where he wants to be but work him even harder.

Keep allowing him the chance to show he's learned the lesson by riding him quietly away again. Remember, if he wants to go back to his friends, hustle him back to them — but then you'll work him until he's begging to stop. You might have to repeat this a few times before you get an improvement but most often, we are pleasantly surprised.

This approach also works in group riding situations, whether your horse gets herdbound when you ask him to ride behind, or over the hill, from his friends. Work him hard around his buddies, then invite him to relax when he's not with them. You might have to set the day up by getting the cooperation of the other riders. It's inconvenient as heck but with most horses, it's only a small part of one day.

Unfortunately, we can build herdboundness by working our horses when we're alone, then stopping and chatting whenever we meet other riders. We end up making the wrong thing fun. If we concentrate on our own behaviour with as much dedication as we do in mastering other horsemanship skills, we'll likely see a changed horse within days.

Remember, success lies in rewarding quiet willingness with gentle, undemanding riding and insisting upon sustained high activity when your horse threatens rebellion. That's all we really need to know. One other thing, a tired horse tends not to be hard to handle. While we're dealing with deep rooted issues like herdboundness, we'll be riding him hard at least five days a week.

Herdboundness is most often a respect issue but it can ramp up according to the weather and even if the horse or pony happens to be a mare in heat, or is experiencing the added stress of a new location. For this reason, plan your 'fix' for a time when it's warm and not windy, or when your horse isn't ruled by hormones. Practice tying him (or her) alone, both at the hitching rail and in the barn. Leave him home alone in a secure pen whenever you're off with the herd mates. Start hauling him everywhere you can, by himself.

Build a trusting relationship where he relies on you for guidance, instead of his friends. These are all good things to help build new mindsets, while keeping you safe. Where we run into trouble is in hoping an insecure horse will suddenly go out and respect our wishes, rather than continuing to make up his own mind. Is it worth it?

Yes! A herdbound horse, no matter how well schooled, has a hole in his makeup that we'll be tiptoeing around until it's addressed. In the end, if your horse isn't getting the message and/or if you're feeling unsafe, it's time to call a pro.

It is important to remember that a very small percentage of horses are so socially and mentally unstable that they cannot or will not be remedied, putting both themselves and their riders in danger when attempts are made to do so. If you suspect yours might be among these, seek a professional opinion on whether or not your horse can be changed. Please, above all else, stay safe.

I'm not all that worried about promises of 'forever homes' when I sell my equine friends and I'll tell you why. I come across many horses and ponies that are in 'forever homes'. Some are good and loving homes, where their people are still interested, still caring for their health, still wanting what's best for the horses, whether or not they are working for their keep.

Some 'forever homes' are purgatories of neglect. Founder, halters left on and making their indelible marks, untreated wire cuts, worminess, poor quality feed, unkempt feet. These horses will never again have someone excited to see them in the morning, dedicated to watching them eat, dreaming of learning things together. They will not be the centre of anyone's life ... and yet, "they will never be sold!" That, more than the thought of them being sent on to new families, saddens me.

When I sell my horses or ponies, I can only do my best to find them the very best people I can. And then, I have to let go. I choose to hope that when my animal has done all he can for his humans, they will either repay him with undying care and appreciation — or find him a new home, with new people who will love and honour who and what he is.

Life goes on. Fortunes change. Good health comes and goes. For better or worse, forever is a very long time.

When I take smaller ponies on, my first conscious thought is that I really have to like them. This isn't always easy if they happen to be demanding, overweight thugs. When days are hard, when progress is falling behind on the random timeline I've imagined (as is inevitable), when they have made me look a fool in public (again), I will need an unwavering belief that it will all be worth it in the end.

My guiding light is to nurture a relationship with these little guys that is every bit as real and meaningful as those with the larger horses that are my friends.

So, how do we build a relationship based on love and respect? This usually means treating others as we would like to be treated ourselves, including the uncomfortable subject of boundaries. We demand respect from ponies, but too often, we fail to respect them ourselves. This is a touchy issue that anyone with talented, quality ponies will immediately recognize.

You have an animal that has been schooled with knowledge and dedication. People, too many judges included, will respond with something like, "How cute is that?!" While generally well meant, it's a remark that doesn't honour the pony, nor the hours of hard work invested. In my opinion, this inability to recognize genuine effort on the part of these little guys is one reason so few ponies go really well.

If our equines, regardless of size, aren't handled with the expectation that they will achieve as much as any good horse, it follows that we will not hold them to very high standards.

Our aim might well be to treat all ponies — all equines — with reverence, to hold them and ourselves accountable in all actions and to find the good in each and every honest try. With such balance, we seldom go wrong … no matter the size of our friends.

Those of us who monetize our passion, must always remember that we are not our work. These words leapt out at me while reading an online article on entrepreneurship recently.

It's all too easy to weigh the highs of sales and others' responses against the lows of not selling, negative comments, financial stress, fatigue and depression. It helps to talk about it with trusted friends when one can. Do we allow our own highs and lows to be swayed by the highs and lows of our business and even of the people following or supporting it? If we're not careful, yes.

One can become downhearted when we begin comparing ourselves to the perceived successes of others, whether they be mentors or competitors. Days when things are hard, we must remind ourselves that our business may be our passion but it is *not* who we are. Then, we must trust that when we share this thing we love, only good will come.

Rain. Not only are we relieved of our fear of fire, but life is brought back to the soil. Frighteningly, our lives become narrow and bleak without it.

A memory of the dry 1980s ... we hear drops on the tin roof of the barn and excited like children, run out to find they are grasshoppers. Rainy day jobs, like an hour spent fixing a broken hinge, or cleaning out the chore truck, do not happen because there are no rainy days. Seven years without rain meant afternoon tanker runs with water for the cows, instead of naps with a blanket and a book. Remembering the stories of old-timers who lived through the Depression, I know the drought of the '80s has changed us, too.

Tonight, should the rain still be pattering on our attic roof, I will lie awake with the joy of it. I will.

I've just been told, "Oh, you flip horses." I guess it depends on your definition of the word flip. We know going in, that well broke horses are not made in thirty, sixty or ninety days ...

Of the last twenty horses to come into my hands, they've averaged two and a half years each in my care. Some of those early rides are scary. To cope, I'm hauling to personal lessons, going to local shows, parades and clinics, plus riding them here at home. Let's disregard the feed, farriers and vet care, or the ones that just don't pan out. I sit down and do the math. Mistake.

When they eventually head on down the road, they take a little piece of my heart with them. Sometimes they come back, under a cloud of shame ... and that's a whole other story.

The bottom line? You've got to do what you've got to do. It all makes sense if it makes you happy.

There's an old saying and it goes like this. "Show me your horse and I will tell you what you are. He is merely a reflection of your commitment, your morality, your strengths, your weaknesses, your hopes and your dreams ..."

One of the reasons it can be hard selling trained horses is that people will buy them and take them home. Soon, there might be a message or a phone call. "Lovely horse," they'll say. Or lazy, or spooky, or moody, or dull and unresponsive. Problem is, whether it's you or me in the saddle, they will reflect us like mirrors. It's enough to drive one to knitting, almost.

You are only as cool as your horse is. While I know this, Henry newly reminds me. We're in the public arena, loping, stopping, changing leads like some well-oiled machine. He's going beyond all imagining. I sit him, feeling smug, doing my best to zone in on the ride but am becoming all too aware of admiring looks being sent his way. There's a particular feeling you get when bystanders like your horse so much, they wish it wasn't you on him.

Fast forward two minutes, give or take. Henry has seen something nefarious going on in the shadows at the far end of the arena. He has told me there's a problem. I bridle him up, "Oh don't be silly", and send him on with my legs. "I said, 'There's a problem!'", he repeats. The next ten minutes are spent with my horse's complete refusal to go anywhere near the dark end of the arena. In his defense, there is something weird going on down there. All of a sudden, I'm driving a tractor with two flat tires and no power steering.

After continued negotiation, Henry finally concedes that his terror is perhaps a false alarm but getting this out of him has not been easy. We're both sweating and short on air. I steal a sheepish glance up at the stands to our band of admirers...

They've all gone home. Wearily, I step off my horse and begin cooling him out. Ego has left the building. Just the two of us, Henry and I are simpatico once more.

IT'S SHOWTIME

"To show, or not to show: that is the question ..."

One of the things that divides horsemen as surely as which discipline we follow, is the old question of whether or not to compete. There are pros and cons to both sides and it's something I wrestle with, myself. Looking back, my most influential teacher absolutely did not put her horses up for judging.

I, however, was blessed to learn from her, and her timeless, classical knowledge has proven to have no bounds. Incidentally, this woman's living was training and selling well-started dressage prospects to household names on both sides of the border. She, who so loved the Thoroughbred, early recognized that Warmbloods were here to stay. Competitive riders were regular visitors to her barn, riders who were more than happy to buy her steeds and head forth into battle. I suspect this upbringing is the model behind my own thoughts.

For much of my life, I've had a competitive spirit. From horse showing to playing Monopoly, I was put here on this earth to win or die. Or so I'd thought. A year or two of life-altering illness did something weird to me and ever since, when it comes to showing, I just don't care.

I've tried to change because I know that the irrefutable fact in the horse world is this: if you are training and selling horses or instructing people, you will be judged by what and where you win. It's called street cred. Like it or not, if we expect someone to part with their pesos, they will want it to be with one who has earned his stripes in the arena. And rightly so — being current, being effective, being successful, is in no way a bad thing.

Today's winners are people we long to learn from, to hold as examples — they mentor us, they help us, they fix our problems, they spur us on to achieve goals, they drive the industry, they allow us our big dreams. They show us everything's possible in horse sport when you mix talent with dedication.

Done well, competition will act as our business card, a proof of our program, a gauge of our own progress. It will teach our children how to lose with dignity and win with grace.

Where the slope gets slippery is when we start having those little conversations with ourselves: that it is normal to pay thousands for this year's show clothes; that our horse needs to be produced this way in order to win; that joint injections are, in fact, healthy maintenance; that we are not serious unless we compete; that breed standards should evolve for the show ring; that it doesn't matter how many young horses are fed into the grinder; that taking our horses for the euphemistic 'tune up' is fine when we don't have the stomach to go after them, ourselves ...

I have ridden out of barns where my underlying feeling, if I'd cared to ponder it, was the rock in the pit of my stomach, an unspoken feeling of dread. These were successful places, barns where anybody would long to ride. They were also places that if the boss was in the arena with the door closed, you backed away. You did not ask questions.

Many of us feel that an achieving horseman cannot claim to be so unless he or she shows. The greater horse industry is built on our collective will to win and I'm all for it, as long as what we're after doesn't cause our horses to self-destruct, mentally or physically. I believe that competition can be done on so many different levels and intensities, that there's something out there for everyone. Or not. We all have our reasons why.

Life with Mike is never boring. Take our recent foray into the entertainment business, a mounted exhibition we were asked to put on for the World Angus Federation. Yes, there really is such a group. Mike, being who he is, jumped at the chance when asked; I'm going on record saying that I would have abstained. This is how I found myself in a mounted wet tee shirt contest, in front of nearly one-thousand people. It gets worse.

My husband, in his trademark enthusiasm for the project, had us decked out in antique western regalia. He wore a smoked buckskin jacket and woolly chaps, with a silver bridle and old high-back saddle for Dan, his trusty steed. I was to be sidesaddle, of course, on Cisco — in a split skirt, silk shirt and scarf with my best hat topping it off. Briefly, we may have looked awesome. As the time drew nigh for our performance, the sky went from merely threatening to a black downpour. And still, the show would go on.

Undaunted, my husband and his horse entered the ring. Cisco and I dutifully followed. I might say that Mike thrives on this sort of thing. He was a radio morning man for many years and to him, nothing in the world is better than the bantering repartee with an audience. Me, not so much. I'd noticed, as I'd ridden in, that my 1880s sidesaddle seemed to be slipping. Further investigation revealed that no matter how much I tightened it, the old leather latigos kept stretching. Oh well, I'd just have to keep my mind in the middle.

We jogged and loped around, did a few turnarounds and got ready to change leads. It was at precisely the same time I bridled Cisco up, that things started going wrong. Horribly aware of the peekaboo nature of my wet grey silk blouse, I kept my elbows chastely at my sides and gathered the romals. Pfft! Pfft! they went, one braided rawhide rein after the other, my workaholic horse loping tirelessly about with dangling bit chains whacking her under the chin. Unfortunately, Mike didn't see any of this, as he was galloping up from behind, preparing his wet rope to make a flashy throw.

"There's a love-knot in my lariat!" sang my everlovin' ham into the headset microphone, calling up his best Wilf Carter, just before the hard, wet rope sailed over my head, smacking me over the nose and pinning my arms to my sides. Still, Cisco loped on. And on. And on. Mike, thinking that I was ignoring him, gave a sharp tug to the rope, in the hopes of getting my attention. Pfft! Pfft! went several of the buttons on my shirt front before I could snarl at him to knock it off.

It was not my finest moment, staying aboard the loosened sidesaddle, trying to suck in my pasty white tummy, fix my hat, tears streaming down my face from the whack of the lariat, Cisco loping, loping, loping... and my cold hands, clutching the dangling reins. Mike eventually 'helped' by hazing her into a corner where, after a few sharp moves, the mare drew to a halt.

You gals would be proud of me, though. After the horses had been put away and all the gear hung up to dry, after a strong drink and a soak in the tub, I was presented with the photographic proof.

To my absolute amazement, I was smiling. Somehow, throughout the whole disastrous affair, every single shot looked as though Miss Congeniality was having a perfect day. Gotta hand it to us wimmin. All hell can break loose and we'll put on a happy face.

Next show you haul your child to, pay attention to how you speak of the judge. Guess what? Judges are real people with feelings — they've crawled out of bed to stand in the hot sun or the wind and rain to not only pick a favourite, but to give your child a helping hand with her horsemanship journey. I've so often overheard parents and children say, "Oh, I hate that judge!" Really? Instead, remember that there are many roads to Rome and the program your family follows, will not be the only one.

Next show you haul your child to, encourage her to say good morning and to thank the judge. This isn't butt kissing, folks — it's called good manners — and learning our manners is a part of good horsemanship, too.

Some days, no matter how hard you've worked, no matter how well your horse is going, the judge just isn't a fan. On such days, it is important to balance your willingness to improve — that is, what you are willing to change in order to win — with a sense of where you are in your program.

If you've shown any length of time at all, you will admit to days when your horse went poorly and you walked out with the trophy. You will remember days your horse went beautifully and you were excused. Such is the stuff of showing. Yes, we must strive always to evolve and do better. But if one disappointing outing has you feeling discouraged, remember your personal goals. Would the horse you rode today beat the horse you rode last week? If the answer is yes, I believe you are winning.

I'm sure that all of us want what's best for our horses. Our circumstances — where we live, where our horses live and yes, what we can afford — have an impact on their care. That said, money spent does not mean a guarantee of excellence when it comes to keeping horses, whether at home or boarding out. It's all too easy to be side-tracked by fanciness, as opposed to what's clean, safe and in their best interests.

I would say that a failure to see is the biggest shortfall in horse husbandry. Is the garbage and old machinery picked up? Are gates hanging straight and swinging freely? Are fences kept in excellent repair? Is the long grass around buildings mowed? Is there a good supply of top-quality feed? Are the pens picked free of manure? Are the water troughs or buckets clean and full? Is there free choice salt? Is used bedding taken well away from the barns? Are the horses content whether in stalls or at turnout? Are blankets regularly changed or reset?

Are buildings well-lit and ventilated? Are aisleways swept and free of rubbish? Is the arena groomed and dust free? Are the teachers and staff professional and friendly? Are safe practices maintained? Are the instructors qualified to teach? Is the barn help well treated? Is morale and the general atmosphere one of calmness and caring, or do you get a sense of hopelessness or resentment when you set foot on the place?

Currently, it is fashionable to skimp when bedding stalled horses. We're told that they're fine on rubber mats but know that a scant shovel of absorbent pellets is cold comfort to a performance horse who might be tired and feeling battered. I believe the best bedding is what is plentiful and affordable wherever one lives. What's more important, to me, is whether our horse can nestle in with enough bedding to cushion his body and block drafts. This is one area where I pay particular attention. The cost and effort required to clean a lushly-bedded stall is minimal if it is picked through twice daily and if the horse gets adequate turn out.

Also, our need to keep aisles clean has somehow become more important than our horses' need to visit, engage in their surroundings and see what's going on. Grilled stall fronts may be beautiful but they come at the price of our horses' souls. One may get a strong sense of a place by walking down the row of stalls and noting the expressions of the horses within. Are they relaxed and pleasant or are they 'inward' and turned with their heads to the back wall?

The secret to equine mental wellness lies in turn out. The closest we come to giving our horses the sense of community and free movement that exists within a herd, the better our horses will serve us and the less complicated and happier they will be. The fewer animals we see pacing nervously, chewing and sucking on fences, the better. Noting the overall condition of an establishment's horses should become second nature. Are they in fair flesh, or too fat or too thin? Overweight horses gorging on round bale feeders are a sign of neglect. Are their coats and feet in good health?

Understand that anyone keeping horses will sometimes have a horse that struggles with his condition, gets sick or is recovering from injury. The question is, what is being done about that? There should be evidence that such a horse is getting the very best possible care and treatment. Teach yourself to scan quickly over a group of horses, to really see beyond an impressive sign or fancy gates.

Finally, the wellness of an equine establishment might be best gauged by how the owners or managers treat the barn help. If the person looking after your horse is overworked, underpaid, labouring without proper paperwork or benefits, is treated with little respect and living in squalor, you can bet that your horses are being skimped on.

This is the dirty little secret of the horse world and once noticed, says so much. Do we argue and demand better? I don't think so. If we've kindly and respectfully pointed to a lapse once and nothing has changed, then we'd best start looking for alternate equine accommodations. Of course, all of this is far easier to see in a public boarding facility than it is to get brutally honest about how we, ourselves, might better care for our horses at home.

The bottom line? I believe the most detrimental thing we do, regarding day to day upkeep, is expecting other people — our children, our trainer, the hired help — to love on our horses and do right by them just because we write the cheques. Our horses are ultimately our responsibility; it is our job to really see how and where they live.

Yet another rider flops down on her horse's back. I watch this and am immediately transported back to my first lesson with my dressage teacher at age fourteen. Only once, she admonished me to "land softly, as though you're setting on eggs".

Sometime later, I was riding alongside another student, when our teacher found herself telling the hapless young lady this, twice. The next day, she asked the girl to get down on all fours once we'd led the horses into the arena. She, a woman of some heft, threw a leg over the girl's back and dropped upon her with all her might. Whompf! Down they went in a cloud of dust, an extreme but albeit effective way of getting the point across.

Ever since, I've been mindful of how I lower myself into the saddle. Many times, people only think of this when they're climbing on colts, 'playing nice' so they don't get piled. Whatever your horse's age, whatever your size (kids can be the worst, so teach them to do better), it is the right way to start each ride.

Effective riding and equitation ... where do you sit?

Ask anyone who rides young horses or performance horses, sitting pretty isn't always where it's at. We don't want our shoulders ahead of our knees, ever. We don't want to hollow our backs. All you hunter seat and western horsemanship people, pay attention: say no to the bubble butt. Our hips have to be ready to ride ahead of our shoulders if necessary, to allow our seat and our intentions to be felt by the horse. All this must be practiced until it is instinctive. Correct equitation is a keystone to good riding, yes, but there comes a point where, if we wish to progress beyond being mere passengers, 'feel' and effectiveness must rise. What I'm saying is, a crotch seat won't get you anywhere.

This brings to mind an equitation championship I watched some years ago. The judge asked the finalists, all excellent riders aged fourteen to seventeen, to canter individually up the centre line and perform an emergency dismount. Only two of the riders were willing to perform the task. The remainder were either in tears or appealing to their coaches to pull them out of there.

I sat there, gripping my coffee, siding wholly with the judge. It was unorthodox but entirely reasonable of him to expect these beautiful riders to know how to safely get away from a wreck. Sadly, they, like too many of us, were schooled only for moments of perfection. This sort of equitation is painted on; it is merely skin deep.

If you are teaching or paying for lessons, remember: there comes a time when sitting pretty isn't enough. We must evolve. Equitation is the basis, the absolutely solid foundation on which to build. As riders, we need the goal of becoming effective: of being able to make adjustments; of knowing how and when to isolate our body parts; of taking a position to actually help the horse.

Whether or not we show our horses, training with pylons is a useful exercise that can tell us more than we care to know. How schooled our horse is becomes apparent when we add precision into the mix. Because I'm generally on green horses, I personally dislike riding with precision and so, must force myself to do so. The pylons tell me how receptive my horse is to my leg in the lope cue, how receptive he is to the neck rein in the circle, how he listens when I ask for a halt.

Remember, relaxation and understanding must come before precision. A correct transition will always be of more benefit to your horse than a pinpoint take off. If you don't have pylons for schooling purposes, painted and water-filled milk jugs will do. Dollar stores sell little six-inch pylons; these are great for leaving in the trailer tack room to run through those increasingly bizarre patterns at the shows … Oops, did I just say that in my outside voice? Darn.

Oprah calls them "Aha!" moments, those split seconds when the fog lifts and you see your own personal truth.

One of mine came during an ordinary sunny morning at the local fair. Having entered my pony in the senior classes, I automatically entered showmanship, too. For weeks, we diligently worked our set ups and pivot turns; I practiced running goofily across the yard all heel to toe, hands level and elbows in (much to the amusement of our farming neighbour, whose fieldwork had him passing our yard) and when the big day dawned, we were more or less ready to strut our stuff.

So, there we were at morning's first light, working our way down a staggering line of competitors. Set 'er up, move into position, stand with tummy sucked in and … move again. The mare, a no-nonsense sort, began to look pained. We made our way through the pattern and inspection and then, back into line for more of it. The judge circled like a shark, back and forth, willing one of us to fall asleep and make a blunder.

And that's when it hit me, the realization that I hated showmanship and as such, had no business even being there. My feet grew roots and refused action. The judge came by and as our eyes locked, he paused and generously waited while I stood my ground. I was done and all but raised my fist to the sky, "As God is my witness, I will never do showmanship again!"

Back at the trailer, I saddled up and poured myself a coffee. The weightlessness I felt was disproportionate to this modest occasion, but for me, the moment was golden. Nothing against all who love this particular class, I vowed that no matter where my endeavours took me, I'd try harder to respect my personal truth.

Schooling and sweating work best in equal measure. Neither works as well without the other. Back in the day, when our family planted cover crops and fall rye, there were soft, worked up fields through the summer, deep enough to get to the bottom of a tough horse. Nowadays, we're not planting cereal crops and it's harder. I've befriended neighbours who plough fireguards around their fields at harvest time and these long, soft runways can work miracles.

The recipe's an easy one. We lope or canter, in long straight lines on a loose rein, asking for nothing, taking no breaks, until the horse or pony asks to walk again. Then, we let him. It's that simple. We don't urge him on, we don't hold him in. In fact, the hardest part is being still and just waiting. If one must be busy, we'll slowly stroke his neck and quarters while he lopes along ...

On a final note, horses can't vocalize or do the primal scream thing. They seem to shed emotion through movement. Perhaps this is why the troubled ones, so often mares, need to lope until they're peaceful. It's another little tool for our tool box.

If you were to ask any parent to name the most important attribute in a child's competition horse, they would say safety first. The reality, however, is all too often something different, something dark. An alarming number of parents will pick winning over being safe. Yes, you read that right. I've encountered this enough to see that the need to parent a winner is so strong, nothing else matters, particularly if friends have put their children on high performance, high dollar horses first.

We're watching parents risk their homes, for God's sake, in order to finance these horses, the training and full board, the diesel trucks and top end living quarters trailers, in order to hold their heads high while they go down the road. The discipline doesn't matter; it's happening in dressage ... over fences ... barrel racing in junior rodeo ... Not only this, parents will often put their child under the tutelage of a toxic trainer, one with questionable morals and methodology, as long as it's a winning barn.

I can't tell you how many times I've watched these scared, pressured kids crash and burn while some other young'un, armed with a huge belief in a less talented horse, blows their wheels off. If not in one competition, then in safe and consistent performance throughout the year, comfortably taking the points race at season's end. And why? Fear aside, this second kid is not saddled with the dreams of desperate parents and in the end, is learning that hard work and undying resolve will, at the very least, hold its own against money's might. For the good of today's youth, so I pray.

One of the things we sometimes forget when we're planning our show-ring turnout is the addition of a smile. We're lucky enough to be doing what we love out there, so don't be afraid to show it.

A bit of advice ...

We find there is no hard and fast rule about where to adjust our bridles. If a pony is bothered or fussy, setting the bit a little higher in the mouth will often comfort her. If we want her to take a stronger contact, we'll likewise set it up. A dull pony often lightens with the bit dropped a hole or two, to the point she's 'carrying' it. To the western folks, it can seem as though the English ponies are smiling up to their eyeballs. Always, the trick is to experiment and see where each pony is at his or her best.

English, western or driving, make sure those top rings on the bit are bent about thirty degrees out for the pony's cheeks. Bits should be made this way but seldom are. Jowly beasts will need them bent further if the shanked bit is to be comfortable. If a pony is fussy despite good dental care, this is the thing we'll check straightaway.

Bits are kept clean. Leather is saddle soaped. We don't have a set rule for curb straps or chains, other than almost always choosing leather. We may even ride a little snugger than most folks do. Many horses and ponies will be less inclined to open their mouths if their curb strap or chain isn't as loose as is often recommended. In Doll's case, comfortably snug is her preference — and "No snaffles, please", she says.

Rather than go with a set dogma of always or never, we just listen to the horse.

Show season is in full swing and there are a multitude of little things that can help you be a winner. I've long been a stickler for beautiful braid jobs and turnout but lately, something has been bothering me a bit about that. When we parents step in constantly, making sure our children are models of perfection, how on earth do we think they'll learn? I guess the question is, do we even care if they learn?

So, here's the challenge: if it isn't a big show, please let your kids rise at the crack of dawn and wind up their own manes. They'll be proud of their efforts and remember, if you must pass judgment, be kind. Judging the local shows, I won't be hard on your child's earnest efforts — braiding is just something we learn to do by doing. I admit as a former horse show mother, I'd do things differently, if given the chance again.

When you're ready to win, you can hardly wait your turn to get out there.

For me, the best way to ensure a good trip is in making sure I don't start trying to fix something that should have been fixed ages ago. If I slip last-minute schooling into the warm-up, it sends us into the ring full of doubt and discord. Remember, show classes are won at home.

Also, I need to look after myself. For me, my mental game is tied in to good nutrition. How many shows have I gone days on bad coffee and French fries — and wondered why I wanted to crash?

How long is your warm up before you show? Whatever our discipline, the problem of leaving our best performance in the warm up ring is all too common. I showed a driving pony for years before I used a stop watch, clicking on at the start of her warm up and clicking off when she was going her best: forward, elastic, happy, 'full of jam'. Guess how long for her to give one hundred percent? Four to six minutes, tops, every single time.

I realized the judges were seeing us waaaaay past our 'best before' date, when she was losing her natural brilliance and getting tired of my nerves. Often, we'd be starting to bicker just before we'd enter the ring. It took a lot of courage to just stop and wait our turn, while the competition was out there, honing their skills.

As soon as I acknowledged the need to stick to our program, the results spoke volumes. Every horse will be different. The flip side, of course, is the horse needing time to settle, the one who doesn't stand a chance when we cut it close and are rushing around.

The solution is to make it a practice to time our horse in different scenarios — at home and away, in hot weather and cold, indoors and out — to find out how long she or he really needs to get 'er done. This year, vow not to leave your winning round in the hitching ring. Nail it in front of the judge!

BACK TO SCHOOL

I got a bit of a scolding, a reminder, at my last lesson.

My teacher was quietly watching me work on an exercise with my new horse. Pilot was kind of getting it but it was harder than either of us had been expecting. He started to resist.

I decided his answer was unacceptable. You could see and feel the horse go from slightly stiff to downright mad in a remarkably short time. Now, it shames me to admit that I can react to anger as though a gauntlet has been cast. I'm all too quick to brandish my sword and challenge you to a duel.

This is a foolish notion when one is sitting on a twelve-hundred-pound horse.

My teacher watched for a moment, while I tried to muscle my way through the rebellion. He gave me time to figure it out. When I didn't, he said, "Get in and get out." What?! Just back away from this display of brute force? Well, maybe.

In two or three strides, Pilot softened. I was able to come back in and ask for a few strides of bend. He answered. I got in and got out again. A few more tries and we were ready to move on to something else.

The moral of the story? While we seldom want to release pressure while the horse is pushing, if the ride is getting emotional, we might choose to move along. We can ask in the next heartbeat, or in another way, or at another point along the time line.

We look beyond the little skirmish, to the far-off end of the war. Sigh. I should know that there's only one rule when it comes to horses …

There. Is. No. Rule.

On 'using the outside rein'.

While the notion of 'using the outside rein' to frame the horse on turns separates the oats from the chaff, there are many degrees to which a rider may do so. The following, which was how I was taught, might be an easier way to understand this concept without so much pushing and pulling.

Whenever we're riding a horse that we're wanting to bring into a state of 'roundness', we begin by picking up the inside rein first, to ask for the bend. This is as simple as raising our inside hand just slightly higher than our outside hand, until we can feel the horse's answer, nothing more. Our inside leg is pulsing at the girth, the outside leg is just hanging quietly, slightly further back.

Once the horse has responded (and we just continue asking him until he does), we want to see nothing more than the inside eye lashes. Then, we'll pick up the outside rein and get a soft feel of the horse, who, if he is 'on the aids' with soft understanding, will start to round up. This is when we can test the use of our legs and the feel we have through our hands and elbows, by a 'giving' of the inside rein.

If we are doing this correctly, the horse will maintain his inside bend but will be working entirely off the outside rein. I would start this at the walk.

To recap, the inside rein asks for the bend. The outside rein asks for the degree of roundness and regulates the forward urge.

By riding with the pulsing inside leg to keep him shaped into the outside rein, we also unwittingly get that 'inside leg to outside hand' that you've no doubt heard lots about. If the horse loses his bend, or his forwardness, we soften our outside fingers and go back to step one, asking with the inside rein first.

As the horse changes bend through a serpentine, we quietly, softly, slowly, change our inside hand by raising and asking for the new bend with it, pick up the outside rein 'til the horse is round and soft, pulsing with the new inside leg, giving with the new inside hand and riding the horse on the new outside rein.

It's fun to see how well the horse maintains his bend into the outside rein, while the inside rein is free of any real contact. The result is that we begin to ride with feeling hands, really aware of what each rein's effect is on the horse.

Our horse will be very light, very willing to keep his own self-carriage, without the crude manhandling that so often accompanies the term 'on the bit'. Always, the inside bend is maintained effortlessly if the rider remembers to hold the inside hand just slightly higher than the outside one, and to ride with softly bent elbows, the arm from the shoulder to elbow hanging perpendicular to the ground.

It takes some practice, mostly to refine our feel but ridden on only the outside rein, the horse will easily keep the correct amount of bend and will be framed beautifully on any sized circle, for any type of transition. By riding with more feel on one rein than the other, the horse will remain soft.

Moments of riding round, always followed by an opportunity to freely stretch down with the head and neck, will ensure the horse develops and maintains a lifelong, healthy build.

Everything — your horse's movement, swing, lightness, obedience, relaxation and joy in his work — is bound to improve. I promise.

Today, I was served up a healthy slice of humble pie at my regular lesson in town. I've been riding a ten-year-old 'colt' for a few months, a mare that's a little skeptical about the notion that life now   with lil' ol' me and sweat-marks and work involved — is better than the previous years spent swishing flies in the breeze. Well, can you blame her?

I'd done a good job of deluding myself into thinking that schlepping around home was setting her up for success... but with the haul down the four-lane, the ensuing hail storm, the PA system, the strange horses loping and spinning and stopping, fencing against the boards, I stepped on and sent her a strong forward message. Doll got humpy and said, "What the ****?!" The lesson here? We're only as cool as our horse is. I spent the night praying and working those one-rein stops.

My horse had been newly prescribed a powdered med that was supposed to be sprinkled on her feed. "Pfft!" said she. Did I mention it was electric blue? I'd been moistening grain and stirring it in with fair results... that is, until the high-energy mare became Jill the Ripper. Stop the bus! It was time for Plan B.

It occurred to me in the middle of the night that I needed only to take some honey, stir the stuff in, load a huge syringe and shoot it into the horse's mouth. Heck, how hard could it be?

Fast forward to me dosing said horse. Syringe seemed plugged. I looked in the small end, then squeezed the plunger firmly, just to see what was bloody well wrong. Ka-boom! Plastered head to toe with dripping, toxic, cobalt honey — I'd got it everywhere, in fact, but inside the horse.

The real fun began in the shower. No, kids, not like you're thinking. I began showering and shampooing and shampooing and showering some more. By the time I'd surrendered, there were cerulean stains on the ceiling, the shower, the tile floor and where I'd blindly felt my way all down the hall. Not only was my blue skin impervious to soap and hot water, our home's painted surfaces resisted cleaning by any known means.

By the way, I never did get any amount of that stuff into the horse. She had the last laugh when, without any help from science, her condition suddenly resolved. Livin' the dream. Yep, I'm livin' the dream.

How tight is your cavesson?

English or Western, I do most of my schooling without a noseband because I want to see and hear what the horse is telling me. If he gapes his mouth open, sticks his tongue out, crosses his jaw, or grinds his teeth, I want to know. If he can't open his mouth, how can I work with him on being more comfortable?

I'm riding a new horse right now whose teeth start chattering the minute he's stressed. Do I put the cavesson on before this becomes a habit, or do I stay the course and see if we can't uncover the reasons why? For me, it becomes more important to find the cause and relief of the horse's stress, than to keep his mouth closed.

As a judge, I am alerted to problems when I see a tightly fitted noseband (anything I mightn't get two fingers underneath). I see an overmounted child, or a hard-pulling horse.

As a rider, I also know that a tight noseband allows the spooky, problem pony to be made more manageable, as constant pressure in one spot dulls the other senses. Just think how a headache renders all other things in our day unimportant. A tight cavesson does the same in 'keeping the lid on' an explosive horse.

As far as stock horses go, when I was a kid, those little bosalitos were called 'mouth-shutters'. Enough said. Working the two-rein is beautiful. It allows one to save the mouth should the cows break or the wheels fall off. It also fills in the hole of the horse that gapes his mouth.

Day to day, old timey traditions notwithstanding, removing the rawhide from the finished bridle horse shows us how he really feels about packing iron. Ever wonder why western horses can't show with nosebands? They hide too many sins.

Bang! Bang! Bang!

I'll hear the clanging of the metal gate as soon as I walk over to feed Tom Jones. Small ponies, especially, are masters at 'speeding up' slow service. They're often just a bit bold about it, impatient and yep, extra smart. It's a common annoyance and easily trained out with some consistency.

I feel for people with stabled horses that paw, then are petted or given treats by well-meaning passersby. Pawing becomes an ingrained behaviour with an instant pay off. A notice on the stall door requesting people to ignore this rudeness is often necessary.

For me at home, it's an easier fix. I do not proceed toward the horse or the feed room while he paws. When he bangs, I stop and drop eye contact, looking as disinterested as I can — and sometimes that's a hard thing when they're raisin' a ruckus. When they stop, as soon as they stop, I calmly proceed either to feed them or let them out for their grazing. They paw, I stop. They stop, I continue. Depending on the willpower and ingrained behaviour of the pony or horse, it's solved without too much fuss.

Where we get into trouble is when we either hurry to stop the horse pawing, or with the attention seeking fellows, start hollering at them or waving our arms.

Such motions from us merely fulfill the desire of these animals to train their people — an exercise where ponies, especially, rule.

What's up with your warm up?

Too often, we lack any clarity when we throw a leg over our pony. Being able to 'roll with the punches' is no reason to forego our schooling goals. At the same time, it shouldn't take forty-five minutes before the pony is able to behave himself, or to perform. We like to think that within about ten minutes, our horse will be ready for anything, both mentally and physically. Here's the plan.

Most horses are clear about whether they prefer to 'whoa, or go'. It's a mistake to think that only the energetic ones need a warm up. If you're going to compete or challenge him in any way, the lazy boy needs to get in the game. We might walk for a minute or two, asking him to bridle up for a few strides, then stretch for at least as many. We want to offer him the reins and have him reach with his nose to the ground.

Once his topline is stretched and he's tracking up with the hind end, it's time to energize and off we lope, first bridling up with a soft feel, then again asking him to stretch his nose towards the ground. Remember that whenever you get a soft feel and some roundness, you must reward by gently 'turning him loose' again. This reward system builds trust.

As soon as the horse is attentive, forward and carrying himself with a stretched topline, we consider him ready. Don't make the mistake of warming up these laid-back fellows for too long.

The nervous or energetic fellow is a little more challenging. Once again, use lots of walk, both bridling up and asking him to stretch. Instead of loping, though, we concentrate on the rising trot. Rhythmic rounding and stretching through the topline are our goals here. This stretching releases endorphins that will soothe and calm him. And yes, occasionally classes must to be missed until the pony is willing to accept our leg without checking out of Dodge. We know we're finally getting somewhere when our high-energy pony needs a wee bit of pushing on.

In case you missed it, the key to the warm up is stretching. Does this come easily? Nope. But stretching through the topline is key to good horsemanship, no matter your sport and one that is skipped all too often, particularly in competitions that focus on collection, that dirty word. If the term 'self-carriage' is of any interest to you, then it behooves your horse to learn to stretch. He will learn to love it.

If, at any time, your arm loses its straight line from the elbow through to the bit, you are not allowing the horse to carry himself; you are forcing his head into position.

To recap, we want a very forward, working trot. We'll invite our horse to stretch and accept the rein, all the way to the buckle. After some nice softening / bending work, we'll gradually 'sneak' up on the reins, just an inch at a time, keeping the energy going and feeling our horse grow round. If he feels resistant, he will be asked to stretch again. A few more minutes — and we'll have our horse moving to his utmost, his head crownpiece high and his weight shifted even further behind.

We can check for this by spotting the convex rounding of the horse's back, behind the saddle, which gives the illusion that he's trotting uphill. A properly stretched horse or pony shows a marked lack of tension throughout the body, especially through the neck, the mouth, the ears. All horses and ponies, especially the lazy, unambitious guys, require this physical and mental warm up before they can seize the day.

Beware the half-broke horse.

We tend to value the quiet fellow, one who never questions or pushes boundaries, but simply goes along and learns his job. The thing is, this guy can become a stranger to stress, that ordinary everyday stuff that vexes us and challenges us to keep our minds in the middle, our feet on the ground …

I recall a western pleasure class full of these slow, quiet horses. They looked really broke. Until, for whatever reason, one of the crowd got humpy and started to buck. Suddenly, the class was full of draped-rein horses that had woken up and too few of them were comfortable with their spiked adrenaline, let alone all this wild 'n' crazy stuff. By the grace of God, no one was hurt.

In an effort to keep calm, many of us try to shield our horses from excitement and misadventure. Unfortunately, we can't control our environs entirely. How our horses handle the pressures of real life is what will ultimately keep us safe. The next time dogs bark or children are playing and you wish they'd stop scaring your horse, I urge you to train him, instead. One day, you'll be glad you did.

Unless you are riding a race horse, speed is not your friend.

No matter the discipline, we see many beautiful horses that would be even more beautiful if they were allowed, or encouraged, to slow down. When the footfalls are rushed, the horse is not able to fully relax. Relaxation is the basis for the horse being able to swing through from behind, to use his body to the utmost, without tension, without a loss of balance, without fear or anxiety. Relaxation comes before rhythm, impulsion or that dirty word, collection.

If you are struggling with your horse: if he is rushing; if he is lacklustre; if he is resisting in some small way; if he is feeling heavy — I encourage you to soften your eyes, your posture, your hands and allow yourself to feel. Encourage your horse to slow down, stretch his topline and swing. This is the basis for all riding; we build on this a little, every day.

You will be amazed and humbled by his transformation, by the beauty of his God-given paces.

Corners. The dictionary tells us that these are "the angles where two straight lines intersect". It also says that to corner something is to "enclose whereby it is hard to escape". Hmmm. Might I add one more?

Corners. These are key to improving your horse.

While I maintain that 'riding out' in open country is hugely important to the education of any safe horse, as much as half the time I'm riding him, I also want to school in an area with four corners and four straight sides. Think 'cereal box'.

Here's why. When I start a green horse, he cannot make the shape of a cereal box. He does not have the body control or the flexibility. Riding this horse will be like riding a dirt bike on an oval track. In fact, as he increases pace, it will feel more and more like "Mr. Toad's Wild Ride". This is normal when a horse, whether young and green or older but unschooled, is learning.

As I ride this horse, I will wait for him to relax and get more rhythmic. This means that he will become more accepting of where I steer him. He will no longer speed up and slow down as he goes around. From the horse's perspective, it's a bit like turning his will over to a higher power. I will ask him to do big, bendy shapes with some circles, some serpentine bends, some tear drops. Always smoothly changing direction, so that he learns to do his work with my brain.

These simple things will be doable for him physically and mentally but they'll still allow me to gain control of his mind and body. The challenge is in keeping a sustained speed, as a green horse is always compelled to speed up and slow down. He does not understand our concept of 'cruise control' and my job is to simply wait it out and guide him.

Once he learns to trust that I will not force him into position or cause him to tip over, he will relax even further. Now, I am faced with choices. I can ask him to slow down by pulling on his mouth. I can ask him to steer better by pulling on his mouth. Or …

I can start asking him to go further into the corners of our cereal box to slow him down, to get him to lighten up and to take some responsibility for how he handles.

I can start asking him to keep his inside shoulder up on these increasingly bendy turns by making sure that I can always, always see his inside eyelashes. This happens whenever I remember to ever-so-slightly lift my inside hand. Magically, without any force, our steering starts to happen with the outside rein.

My goal, in addition to riding round circles and equally bendy turns, is to ride my horse around the perimeter of the area, using four straight lines and four corners. This is easier said than done. Doing so requires a horse who is obedient, who listens to the outside rein, who listens to my inside leg, who adjusts his speed and balance to go into a turn and again, when coming out of it. Doing so means that I am riding an increasingly well-schooled horse.

This is not news. Those of us who've shown rail horses have long known that the person who controls the corners in a big class is the person who controls the rail. This is the horse who appears to be going slower but more rhythmically than any of the other horses, even if he's not the best one.

Each lap of the ring, he has four excellent chances to reset and rebalance. We know that the horses and riders who 'use their corners' are the ones who are in it to win it.

The next time you are training in an enclosed area, start gently requiring yourself and your horse to ride the entire cereal box. This won't come overnight but once you are mindful, it will gradually, magically happen.

Doing this one little thing will see your horse hugely improved.

We have a horse who doesn't do something well — and the hardest thing is in working on that one little thing. It'll be something simple — like standing for saddling, or waiting in the trailer — and we think, he doesn't do that very well, so I'll not push it.

Wrong. That one little thing just needs practice — not perfect practice, but getting a little better each time practice. Human nature has us wanting to work on what we already rock, rather than the thing that makes us uncomfortable. But when we calmly meet that little 'hole' head on, it is always a surprise to find that the rest of the horse improves.

I had a young, green horse out in public, a horse I wanted to get some time on in an indoors group, as most of my miles are made outside and alone. We had steering and control — or so I'd thought — but as one rider after another kept passing us too close for comfort or worse, tail-gating, I began to wonder if I'd made a mistake.

When one gal on a finished bridle horse actually loped a large, fast circle outside my slower, smaller one and our stirrups hit, all hell broke loose. We got by, but it took a fair bit of time before my gelding could focus around other working horses, without going into self-preservation mode. I've gone so far as considering tying a red ribbon in his tail to warn people off but that seemed silly as he's never kicked anyone in his life. Yet.

I realize that if you've never started a colt, or made a green horse, it's easy to forget that not everyone is sitting as pretty as you are. It's a small kindness, however, to hold off the cantering until the colt has been mounted and is trotting out; to keep a few horses' lengths when you're following; to pass wide when you want to swing by; to keep your eyes up and stop, if and when the youngster goes to bucking; and to avoid fencing, sliding stops and hard turnarounds close by me, until you see how we're going to cope.

Your payoff will be my undying gratitude — along with a young horse who will feel confident enough to come back and do it all again. This careful observation won't be needed forever, I promise, but having it *is* good horsemanship.

For saddling, I like the horse to stand untied, for our mutual safety and in teaching manners. Yes, he'll be haltered but the lead rope will just lay over my arm. Nervous horses can move their feet a bit and avoid a blow-up. Bored horses who shift around and paw while tied can learn to ground tie and assume responsibility for their own feet.

There's a meme floating around that says, "I love my horses too much to tie them while I saddle!" — a bit of cowboy pomposity that disregards the lot of well cared for, high-achieving horses from other realms. We live in a world where our horses often must stand tied, hobbled or cross tied for saddling. If we really love them, we'll prepare them for that, too.

The walk tells all.

We, as people, get bored and impatient. We are in a hurry, running late, paying for good riding time or have only an hour ... and we will make excuses to ourselves. Worse, very few show classes really celebrate the walk, or put enough emphasis on the quality of this most important of paces. Why is it so key to the quality of a horse or the thoroughness of his training? Because the walk tells all.

Dressage scoring gives the free walk a coefficient of two, which means that the mark of this movement is doubled when calculating the final score. The walk is the basis of all training. It is hugely important as it is all too easy to make rushed walks, pacey walks that do not have an even footfall of 1-2-3-4 — there will be an emphasis on the second and fourth beats, for instance — as well as horses that are not clearly overstepping the front foot prints with the hinds. Horses that cannot swing along and down at the free walk are showing holes in their training, where the stretching and building of their toplines have been skimped on, where the rider's hands have played too large a part.

So, what can we really do to help? Fixing a walk is not hard per se. It is constant and mindful, which makes it a challenge in itself. If you're still skeptical, a horse that improves his walk will greatly improve in his trot work and canter, too.

When I am picking a horse to buy in the first place, I am looking for the horse that swings along at a walk, really overstepping with the hinds, whether loose in turn out or being led in hand. Such a horse is blessed to begin with and my job is then in keeping his walk beautiful, despite my training. The horse that shuffles along or paces is a different story. I am going to have to be very mindful in my riding with this horse, allowing him to walk in a slower cadence while stretching to the bit, then teaching him to swing with my legs alternating in rhythm as he strengthens, stretches and understands.

When do horses naturally walk best? When they are tired after a day in the saddle and we set them to walking home. This is when we can get them to settle into the task, to learn to love a free walk with loose reins swinging from side to side. In fact, those swinging reins are a huge sign that the horse is using his entire body to get the very best walk he can. After a few miles of this, he will be rhythmic, swingy, driving from behind, never jiggy or rushed. This, alone, is a good reason to get show horses out on the trails. Western rail horses that are jogged too much will show a deadened walk, as well.

Back in the arena, or riding in the field, let's bring our horses soft and round for a few steps, then work at lengthening for a few steps, then bring them 'round again, then really walk out as much as they can on a loose rein ... always changing, always challenging, always investigating the different degrees of the walk. Our horses learn that there are many types of walk, that they are all beautiful and enjoyable and that walking well is not a waste of time.

Sometimes, we need reminding that when it comes to the quality of horses, to the wellness of our horsemanship: The walk tells all.

Here's an important word when it comes to riding: sustain. Sustain. Ride long enough to let the horse settle at the canter or the lope, or stand on a loose rein as a reward, or really march along at the walk, or whatever. So many people will go four or six strides, then stop, then off they go again, all in fits 'n' spurts. These riders have been told that transitions will improve their horses but in my experience, these are just as likely to irritate a horse and erode his confidence. I'd far rather let my horse settle into what he's being asked to do, to get moving rhythmically, to breathe. Transitions are more a test, a tool, once the gait is established.

Curves and changes of bend are lovely but always, the horses are asked to sustain their gait, much like driving at a steady speed along the highway. In my mind, the ability to stay on cruise control, no matter the gear we choose, is one big thing separating a well-trained horse from a green one. It's the difference between feeling comfortable and feeling dodgy.

Until we learn to sit it out, to wait, the horse will never be able to let his guard down and just master this one thing. And by adding one little thing to another little thing, he becomes a relaxed and beautifully schooled horse.

Of all the horse training tools available, the best one might still be the wet saddle blanket. For some reason, it's got a bad rap these last few years, as though making a horse work for his living is somehow abusive.

Along these same lines, I don't advocate turning sweat-marked horses out to fend for themselves. But when my horse or pony finally has his light bulb moment, I step down. Right then and there, I pull my tack. Will I have to walk him out? Or will my precious riding time be cut short? Maybe.

Remember this: when it comes to positive reinforcement, our actions speak louder than words.

When it comes to setting our horses and ponies up for success, we always recommend saddling them for at least half an hour before riding. Why? Well, most horse wrecks happen during the first few minutes of the ride. If our horse is saddled somewhat loosely, tied and left to think and stand quietly, it allows his mind and back to 'warm up' before anyone climbs aboard.

We never just tighten our saddles and swing up but move the green horses' feet around a bit, either on a long rein or in a 'ground driven' circle. Older horses are turned around to face the other way, once or twice, 'unlocking' them, if you will. Should you have to do this on a well broke horse? Heck no, but it's a good habit to get into, all the same.

This is old-fashioned, out of date thinking from Grandfather's era — and like many such remedies, bears consideration, no matter the saddles we ride. This quiet and gradual saddling and cinching up is also the best way I know to help rehab a cinchy horse and to prevent it, in the first place.

Asking the horse to soften.

If I think about the horses that I've adored spending time on, they were horses with a marked lack of resistance. Please don't confuse this with mental brow-beating.

'Soft' horses have a serenity to them that brings to mind the dancer trained in ballet. They have immense body control, they can isolate body parts to respond to us and they have a mental preparedness that allows them to sail through life gracefully. Soft horses have had someone in their lives who have taken the time to make things right.

We know that any lightness 'up front' must originate from the source of power that lies behind the saddle. That said, it can help the horse with his understanding if we can ask him to soften to the left, and to the right, at the halt.

We play a bit with this. We keep our requests loving, slow, gentle. How little 'feel' do we need to get an answering response? If we lighten our hand, does the horse snatch it back, or does he offer to stay soft? Is one way much less resistant than the other?

Then, we ask these same questions at the walk. The left rein for a few strides, then the right, then we repeat. How is he feeling? As long as our horse has a stiffness that is unchallenged in this simple exercise, he will have a resistance through his body whenever we pick up both reins, and especially through transitions.

This is not a sawing motion on our part but a soft hold, a request, until he releases. Our response is to immediately soften. Use only one rein at a time. For clarity, the other rein must hang without demand.

By the way, most of us need to mindfully tell ourselves to 'slow down our hands'. We humans are wired to be grabby. I never tie my horse's head back to the saddle, or use side reins or draw reins, because I want to train my horse to respond to live touch, to a feeling — and not to force.

English or Western, this left to right to left softening exercise is something that can start any ride. It's a gentle way to flex out stiffness from a 'going' horse, if he's feeling bracey after hauling, or if he's had an awkward night in the stall. Likewise, it's a pleasant start on the greener horse. We can slow things down and quietly communicate.

It reminds our horse where we are coming from, what the correct answer is — and like yoga — gently warms up the mind and body for what is yet to come.

Spooky horses.

There must be a lot of them, as more people write in about shying and general jumpiness than just about anything. The biggest problem with these guys is that they are very good at undermining our confidence, chipping away at it, bit by bit.

Human nature has us wanting to protect spooky horses by carefully controlling the environment so that they don't go off the edge. This is akin to trying to sneak by the sleeping giant. You can never let your guard down and when something does get by your careful screening, his wheels will fly right off. So, what to do?

While some horses might have physical problems that feed into this — sore backs or poor eyesight, for example — most horses with this behaviour just have a fear-based make up. If you add high energy to their lack of bravado, you're in for a wild ride. Many spooky horses are also manipulative; they'll get you dealing with a shy, rather than putting them to work. Any sort of a reaction from you invites them, too, to react. "You scared me!"

Sound familiar? Wrapping them up in cotton, trying to force the world around you to not make noise, almost guarantees failure. The only thing left is to desensitize them. You can explore different techniques, such as flooding them with stimuli or taking part in bombproofing clinics, but one method that works well for me is to simply step off and start my chores.

I'll put a rope halter on the horse, one he'll not tow me around with, along with a rope lead. Now, this is important: I'll check his respect for my personal space, making sure he steps back whenever I face him, as well as teaching him how much 'bubble' I need to be content. I don't want to get run over just because this guy doesn't like the looks of my garden hose.

Then, I just go to work. I might roll the wheelbarrow out to pick pens or tidy the arena, letting the horse trail along with me on a slack lead rope. We might rake gravel off the lawn, or water plants, or pick rocks, or sweep the aisle. Point is, by putting my focus on the job at hand, I take a lot of pressure off my horse. I always know where he is behind me, so that I can stay safe but I won't worry too much if he's not liking what I'm doing. I'll just keep chugging along.

Changing direction, chatting away, making strange sounds, puttering about, he learns to follow me and not get stressed out by things he doesn't necessarily like or understand. If he starts crowding me, I won't get too bugged by it; I'll just change direction and go back to work.

This sounds really stupid but it's worked wonders for years, including with herdbound behaviours ... and I don't have to wish I was a better bronc rider or a horse whisperer, to boot. Often, the process takes as little as an hour or so, before I start seeing a big improvement in how he handles scary stuff, both on the ground and when I ride.

By simply plugging away at a few of the endless little jobs that pile up around every farm, I lose track of my frustrations and training woes, I forget about watching the clock and looking for improvement ... and my horse learns to enjoy being part of an elite team that gets things done.

"For goodness sake, Pilot's ten years old!"

Yes, I know. When we start our relationships, all the horses and ponies that come here — and not just Pilot — go back to square one. It's not the same as starting a colt from scratch. We'll move fairly fast if all is well — but we make darned sure our house is built on a firm foundation.

Does he stand quietly and without moving while I groom and saddle him, the lead rope over my arm? Does he move fluidly — stretching down, breathing evenly, relaxing, chewing, keeping his shoulders up at walk and trot and canter — while on the lunge? If not, there is little point in my being on top of him until he understands.

This slow approach is twofold: it gives a new horse confidence and it keeps me safe. With a few minutes of lungeing, I stop Pilot, check the softness in his face and step on. Only now is he ready and willing — and age has nothing to do with it.

'Knowing when to quit' and having an 'attitude of gratitude' may be the two biggest things in our training tool box. The day-in, day-out slog magically feels better when we're shown some appreciation. Trust me, our horses and ponies feel the same.

I love this quote from Eric Barker, author of *The Upward Spiral:* "It's not finding gratitude that matters most; it's remembering to look in the first place."

The subject of showing very young performance horses became one of the most controversial postings yet on the Keystone Equine Facebook page. While I'm not a fan of this lucrative backbone of the horse industry, I'll admit that I like seeing young horses started in the autumn or winter of their two-year-old year. Why? Despite heated protests — I can hear them now — these youngsters get a chance to learn about submission and respect while their minds are open to suggestion. They get a start that allows them to feel their way along and progress at a slow rate without anyone getting scared or in a fight.

Older ponies and horses can be a whole other can of worms. Having brought in a fair number of aged, spoiled ones over the years, I can tell you with absolute certainty that an unstarted colt will progress and hold onto his newfound knowledge a lot quicker and happier than will a mature one with habitually bad behaviours. A really immature colt that doesn't seem ready to be ridden can still be taught to stand tied, saddled and bridled and learn to pony out.

I personally don't like to drive youngsters in the carriage without at least one year of under saddle work. The chances of getting in a wreck are so much greater in harness and the mental damage to a young runaway can be irreparable. Note that with very small ponies, we'd start them in harness out of necessity, rather than begin their education in the hands of a child.

Allowing for differences in temperament, the easiest ponies are the ones who have learned respect during colthood and not at age ten. Foals can be halter broken and taught to give of their feet. Please don't over-handle those youngsters!

Improper imprinting and familiarization at a young age are very difficult to overcome if your goal is a sensitive and responsive horse. After weaning, the youngster should know how to lead and tie up, stand tied for his supper, have his feet handled and accept grooming. He will know whoa! Aggressive or high-energy youngsters are ponied cross country from a rock-solid horse, keeping their minds busy and teaching respect.

By late age two, they will know just enough about lungeing or round penning to go quietly and change direction, read our body language and accept the saddle and bridle, along with a rider, too. By three they'll be ridden, indoors and out, at walk, trot and lope, for short durations of about twenty minutes, tops. No headsets, no drilling, just an understanding and enjoyment of the working life. From then on, it's smooth sailing.

We reckon that young horses and ponies shouldn't be carrying much over twenty percent of their body weight — and don't forget to figure in your saddle when you tally the pounds. We never see popped splints or other injuries, as we do most of our early riding at a free walk, up and down the hills. Our horses muscle up through their backs and haunches and learn to really problem-solve. This slow and quiet program continues on through their third year and just gradually steps up to include more athletic endeavours at age four and beyond.

Can aged animals be just as willing to learn, to suddenly have meaning and purpose in their lives? Absolutely. I believe it completely. But a word of warning: they can also be downright dangerous. Horses and ponies that have buffaloed people in the past tend to get mad when faced with opposition, particularly those older mares. Also, the longer a pony is left before training commences, the more we deal with issues of herdboundness.

If this sounds like a familiar situation, I'd recommend professional help. Meanwhile, vow to start your younger ponies on an ideal upbringing for happy, healthy, long and useful lives.

Swishy horses.

We've all seen them; many of us have also owned and ridden them. While there are many reasons that a horse might swish his tail while working, it has been my observation that some horses seem prone to this, even while loose around others. Once a horse exhibits a busy tail, it's easier said than done to school it out of him.

Causes are varied and, I think, most often point to some sort of discomfort, whether this unease is a physical or purely emotional one. Mares have a reputation for being swishy and I think many are working with sore backs, due to both their longer conformation and their heat cycles. Mares tend also to be more sensitive than the boys along their sides, requiring extra compassion when girthing, as well as light and knowledgeable leg aids.

I would suggest that any horse, regardless of gender, who swishes his tail when cued with the legs, is either uncomfortable or is somewhat soured. Often if we can get them doing a change in jobs, or working in a different environment, the problem is greatly reduced. It is imperative that no matter what, the horse is deemed sound by a vet and/or chiropractor and is put to work under a saddle that fits. Ulcers and downhill conformation are just two common factors.

In my experience, the swishy horses have generally been the friendly ones who have ended up feeling put upon and misunderstood. Perhaps they were rushed in their schooling, or were pressured when they didn't quite understand. They have lost much of the joy in their work. It interests me to note that very few driving horses exhibit busy tails and that the issue seems largely to exist in horses that are ridden in all disciplines.

I've had the best luck with swishy horses by taking my spurs off and using a long dressage whip to back up my leg aids. I'll cue lightly, then if I am ignored or swished at, I'll cue strongly, just once, with the dressage whip right behind of my active leg. This gets the point across.

I am never interested in tying or deadening the tail in order to mask what my horse is trying to say. Much as it hurts to admit, my swishy horses are most often telling me to be a better rider.

On being a teacher, on being a student …

I know now that I have always wanted to be both of these. While seemingly polar opposites, each is an equal part of who I am. There's a bit of vulnerability in admitting this because if you are a teacher, it is assumed you know it all and that you shouldn't still be casting about with an empty loop. If you admit to being a student, then who do you think you are to aspire to teaching, to sharing what you know? These are but two of the things I tussle with whenever I whack myself upside the head with self-doubt.

Always, the horse world is a great parallel to life. There will be sharp turns and dead ends along the road to wherever it is we're going. Yes, there will be those who rejoice in our downfalls but if we hold tight to the spirit of learning, then our failures become keys in our success, a way of finding the paths we're meant to tread. I know that if I am to teach well, I need to keep on with my own learning.

If I'm wise about choosing those who mentor me, they mightn't tell me what I long to hear but they'll shore me up in areas that need strengthening, the places I feel most vulnerable and weak. These key players become one's treasured support system. Living or dead, I count perhaps three teachers who have stirred together the strange mixture that is who I am. Whether it was forty years ago or just last week, studying with them has offered no shortage of opportunities to grow.

We riders will make our own mistakes (also known as lessons learned), go down random avenues, weather a few regrettable storms. There is no reining around them. I am learning — I am teaching — that no matter what, we will dust off our boots, pull down our hats and carry on.

NOTES

NOTES

AUTUMN
Reflection

Summer, I have loved you. How can you be gone so soon?

As close as summer is to my heart, I have learned that these next months are the year's most glorious. The air intoxicates. By the time our landscape is changing to her autumn palette, I, too, am ready. I long for comfort food, the richly-simmering soups and stews. I love wrapping myself in warm woolens and quality, classic clothes. Everything about fall is a rich tapestry and our daily grind becomes somehow more sumptuous.

Some of us will admit, deep down, that while we're a little afraid of the spectre of winter, we're relieved to have made it past summer's glaring heat and flies. We're not supposed to say so, but it's another wonderful thing, having our kids back in school. And so, we ride.

Some of us are looking toward the year's biggest competitions, the pinnacle of all our efforts, our blood, sweat and tears. Others among us head for the trails. As a rancher's wife, I was a late convert to the magic of going to the mountains. I'd spent my days in the saddle, in cold wind and open country ... and after each of them, I was grateful to kick off my boots and spurs, finding solace in the bathtub. What I was missing, of course, was that my days spent riding were at my place of work. I was missing out on play. It took an elderly friend who had grown up in these mountains to make me accept this. Autumn, in all her glory, was waiting for me along the mountain trails.

Fall's minor chord makes her a time for remembrance. We think of the people we knew and the horses we trusted. Days we were on top of the world ... and days when we couldn't draw breath for the heartbreak. The joy of horsemanship is found somewhere between our greatest highs and the valleys where we can feel no lower. In the end, our memories are what we'll have left of a wonderful way of life. To remember them is good.

HAPPY TRAILS

I love driving trucks and hauling horses.

While other gals get their fill from jewelry and hot spot vacations, I crave a clean truck and trailer, windows and wheels shining, driving tunes on CDs. Settling in on a recent haul, I notice a shadow running parallel to the highway. It's the old road, now grassed over, with stone and cement abutments at each coulee where once there were bridges. I crane my neck to see: 1910. This ghost road runs alongside for miles, criss-crossing the new highway but never quite in the same tracks.

Swathers, combines moving, kicking up dust for miles.

I skirt a stolid Komfort Koach, still singing, still listening to voices past. Tormented trees make a line on the shortgrass and even the cows here have dead-looking coats from the wind. Have I, in some former life, lived in one of these leaning houses that would have flown away, had it not been tied down? Oilcloth curtains, dust drifting across the floor … What years did the grasshoppers come? I can't remember … was it before or after the baby died? Imagination wrestles reality as I slow and make the turn north on Highway 36.

Thank God, I can leave. Peeling signs point to the ball diamond, liquor off-sales, a cemetery. Then, deep into a vast John Deere empire, I pull off for a Coke and some fuel. "Can you help me?" asks a shy, young woman wearing a homemade scarf and long polka dot dress. Keeper of maybe six children and a new Cadillac Escalade, it is soon apparent she cannot read. How, why, here, now, can this even be?

Overcome with these questions, I push buttons at the prompting of her gas pump, then escape onto the highway, behind a Ram Tough truck and a purple ragtop. My heart full to bursting, with one last guitar chord, I cross the Bow River and weep.

Another day of handling horses in that keening southeast wind and I'm left edgy, short of breath and with a weird sense of impending doom. Apparently, the wind blows unsettling messages into my ears, as well as those of the horses ... Or is it just me?

Many years ago, our mountain horses had a hard time adapting when our family moved to the wide-open prairies. Distances were so vast and the wind was a constant presence. Some days, the incessant howling in their ears would literally drive them mad.

The opposite, we have also found to be true. Horses taken from rolling grasslands to the bush will take about three days to come apart at the seams, going all the way from well-broke and chilled, to mentally unrecognizable. Mountain and bush horses have learned to cope with that closed-in feeling, moose and bear sign, the wind soughing in the jack pines, endless hills, bogs and deadfalls to negotiate, along with a super race of mosquitoes.

If you're buying a horse from an entirely different ecosystem, especially if he is to work on trails or the ranch, be very patient and understanding of this process. People often have the same reactions — particularly if they have sensitive, highly strung natures — and some never are wholly able to adapt.

Here's a concept I will hammer home until my dying day. Good horsemanship is NOT breed or discipline specific. If I hail from the pricey worlds of the pony hunters or the breed show pleasure horses, I am a little different — but no better — than the lonely soul out schooling the off-track Thoroughbred, or the guy in Wranglers heading down the fence to turn a cow.

We hear too many comments from one crowd about how badly mannered the horses are in another, or the righteous condemnation of everything from bits to shoes. Each branch is somehow convinced their discipline is the 'truth', requiring far more skill and insight than any other on the same tree.

Now, some of my own prejudices stem from feeling that certain disciplines border on abuse. That's a tough one and I still don't know what to do about it. I do feel, however, that my own ignorance will not do anything to help the animals I love. So, I must learn more. Certainly, with every decade, I see fewer and fewer trainers who know how to school a jumper, AND put a horse onto a cow, AND drive a Hackney in a viceroy, AND train and present a show hack.

It's a long list of things my mentors of old just knew. So, what the heck has happened to general knowledge?

Today, let's vow to appreciate quality, caring horsemanship that has the horse working happily and confidently at his job — whoever it is, wherever it is, whatever it is. I dare each of us to go beyond that place where the tack and the price tags are colouring our thoughts.

Despite a horrible some-sort-of-fruit-sized hailstorm, fire, wind and other natural calamities, the local rodeo queen contest went ahead as planned. What fun to be included as one of the judges.

Seeing as these gals were more glam than I will ever be, I could only comment upon their grace in the saddle and pick one who displayed the best cowboy-up mentality whenever the wheels fell off. And you know what? My mother was right all along. No matter what your horse is doing, baby, you've still gotta smile.

In my neck of the woods, the woods are incredible right now. The colours, the piercing quality of the air, the joy of riding without flies … Autumn is always the best time for riding here on the eastern slopes of the Rocky Mountains.

One day, I will wake up and know that this is it. I will pull out my eiderdown coat, I will catch and saddle and feed my horse and then, I will pack a lunch and call a friend. There's nothing like a few hours on the trail, jackets now shucked and tied on behind, stopping the ponies and while they graze, hobbled, opening up the wonder of our packed lunch. We'll sit and philosophize among the mason jars of lemonade, hard-boiled eggs and strong cheese, wondering why we don't do it again and again …

We never do. Winter comes and catches us napping but there are no regrets.

Do I have a mantra while riding these guys? You bet I do. Three words, said over 'n' over. Love and rules. Love and rules. Love and rules.

Coming on Strong: The Dark Side of Natural Horsemanship.

My opinion on this subject might offend a few folks but still, it needs to be said. The term 'natural horsemanship' is a relatively new one in the horse world. There have been untold generations of animals that have successfully negotiated the working and competition worlds without ever having seen a flag or a round pen. That said, there are benefits to the process, provided the handler has a working knowledge of how and why he is using pressure and release and provided he has a genuine sense of feel and timing.

Unfortunately, none of the above can be learned by reading books or watching videos — and few of us have the ability to change ingrained patterns of a lifetime by attending a clinic. The result is a handler who knows 'just enough to be dangerous' and the price, of course, is paid by you know who.

When buying horses, I'm simply looking for animals that live in the middle ground between begging for cookie love and having had the you-know-what flagged outta them in the round pen. When horses are veering between these two extremes — and too many of today's horses are — they are a dangerous mix of scared and mad.

The premise of natural horsemanship boils down to getting respect. With some horse owners, this works beautifully. With others, it doesn't and there's a generation of highly offended, aggressive horses out there. I'm seeing horses so wrongly trained to come to us, they'll chase their owners right out of the pen.

I am suggesting that many of us close our natural horsemanship books and go back to basics. Be polite, say "how do you do?" in a friendly fashion and slowly, quietly, get to work. We may laud the three-day colt starters — but there are NO substitutes for wet saddle blankets, long miles and the passing seasons. There are no short cuts. The average horse will be happy to give you his loyalty and respect, provided you earn it and are not what he considers an ill-mannered boor.

If you still want to be a natural horsemanship trainer, then do your homework. Weed out the shams from the good guys, then apply for a learning position with someone who knows how to get it done. Remember, round penning is a means to an end, one little tool in making a working horse. All too often, it's an endless purgatory from which there is no escape.

Loosen up.

Of all the spoiled beasts we bring in, many are cinchy to the point of being dangerous. This habit ranges from pinned ears, cow kicking and tail swishing, all the way to pulling back, lying down and rearing over backwards when saddling. Most people are shocked when they learn this vice is man-made.

When your horse is first saddled, the cinch should feel no snugger than the waistband on a comfy, slouchy pair of pants. We only pull it tighter right off the bat on a colt that might buck, as we don't want the saddle to end up underneath him. On a horse that's waiting tied, or going to be trailered, the snugness mentioned is more than enough. It takes three or four gradual tightenings and moving the feet around to 'cure' a cinchy horse — and to keep him thus.

The cinch is always loosened a bit when we step off. With this fair treatment, a habitually cinchy horse can be cured in days. He'll revert very quickly with rough handling, though. Many horses become cinchy during the winter because their long coats and soft, flabby elbows get caught up. We have to watch out for this.

Lastly, and this is important, if you oil or soap your latigo, it will need jerking to tighten. A dry latigo slides smoothly and when it's past its prime, just throw it out. Mares, especially, resent thoughtless handling when saddling. Interestingly, this problem seems to be a Western thing. Do English riders tend to be more gradual when girthing up?

If a horse doesn't improve within days, we look at chiro or wonder about ulcers. Dosings of aloe vera juice can be magical. Finally, if nothing alleviates the pony's cinchiness, it's time to check the pecking order and our rank.

We are often asked what the secret is to consistently putting good ponies out there? Well, here it is, so sit up and pay attention: it's adults. Adults train the ponies! Behind every rock-solid horse or pony, no matter his size, is a committed rider with skills and experience. For most people, these things are only attained with age.

Kids are great but they're not horse trainers. Every champion pony I know has an adult in his life who isn't too proud to get on and set him straight.

Curiosity may have killed the cat but it is a very good thing for the horseman.

When I really think about it, most of the times I've got jaded, or stopped being open in both my mind and my heart, it's because I've grown set in what I think. When I feel 'right' all the time — and golly, it's so easy to do — I stop handling and working my horses with openness. My friendly Q&A format morphs into a long list of demands.

I'm getting into dangerous territory when I feel as though I'm working as hard as the horses. Soon, all the joy is lost, both for me and most assuredly, for them.

By wanting to know the hows and the whys behind all of what we do to evoke their responses, we might start considering our time with our horses and ponies as a challenging game, more like a quest for knowledge.

"How can we figure this out together?" we might ask. Or, "How can I make your job better?" Best of all, curiosity is catching. The horses invariably mirror our enthusiasm and next thing you know, our days grow rich with possibility. Searching, inquiring, asking our horses questions … This, alone, can turn the ordinary into something special.

Whenever I am asked to help someone find a horse, I reply that I would love to, because I know that it's a jungle out there. First, however, both as a lifelong student and a sometimes teacher, I would urge: please, first of all, ask your coach. If you value your instructor's knowledge enough to take lessons, it's natural that you will trust his or her judgment when horse-hunting, too. When your teacher matches you up with a suitable horse, it will be able to transition effortlessly into the new program and to your riding style — and you know it will be liked.

I suspect that most reputable sellers will welcome your teacher to come along with you, but make sure that what's been advertised is actually something your coach is keen on trying. So often people will buy a horse without their instructor's blessing, showing up at the barn with a surprise horse from someone else's program. It's not fair to you, it's not fair to the teacher; it's sure not fair to the horse.

Training alone is a unique place where one rides a fine line between being brave and staying safe. I very recently caved in to family pressure, carrying a phone so that I might call for help if I get in a pickle ... although that would mean putting the blessed thing in my pocket and not leaving it at home when I ride.

Seriously, though, when I'm alone, I admit to proceeding a little differently ... always letting people know where my path might take me, always making sure I can kick free in a pinch, always being aware of not biting off a little too much in case things get carried away. Let's face it, this is always a possibility, as I often work green and dodgy horses.

The upside? When I train alone, I am freed from my ego — my horses get the real me, every single time. The downside? There is always a little voice that says "stay safe, don't rock the boat, maybe save this for another day". It makes me a more conservative/chicken rider but turning my back on Ego is a pretty good thing, when I really think about it.

There are those who say I am foolhardy. I say these admonitions do not wash here, nor do they for legions of riders who just go out and do the job every single day. When one works alone, bravery can be little harder to come by — but this caution is a natural preservative, especially as we age.

If we're asked to ride our horses around other peoples' cattle, we always have to stop and think. Cows and horses just naturally go together. Cows will teach our horses way more than we ever could. The problem is, will what they teach our horses be for their good?

A day that sticks uncomfortably in my mind happened recently. I was putting time on a green mare who was working and watching nicely when we got a request to gather and trail a neighbour's herd home from their summer pasture. Mike and I blithely loaded up and set out. Mistake! These cows — farmers' cows, we call 'em — had, in living memory, only been handled with quads and weren't about to take any nonsense from the likes of us. They'd got through life outrunning their handlers, doubling back and threatening aggressive action.

Suddenly, it was hard riding just getting these girls gathered and I ended up doing a fair bit of running and pulling on my horse. At one point, she got T-boned by an old cow who didn't buy in to our nonsense. In mere minutes, I felt my confident mare turn into a puddle of self-doubt and confusion. I kicked myself. I should've been on an old timer who had pretty much seen it all, one who wouldn't get scared or chargey if things turned western. As it was, I had weeks of slow, thoughtful riding just getting the mare dialed back in around cows.

Can spoiled cattle be rehabilitated? Yes, with knowledgeable handling, good horses, better dogs, and an understanding of bovine pressure and release. Such cows are not the cows to school young horses on, however. For that, we look to cattle that have been handled slowly and correctly by horsemen. We can almost guarantee these cows will walk quietly from A to B and will head up (stop) whenever we reach their tipping points.

Even with new calves at foot, they will respect us. These are the cows that will train our green horses to quietly do the job. They will teach our horses to think first and react later. They will give our mounts the confidence that is so vital in making them good workers. We also avoid handling yearlings with green horses whenever possible, as these 'teenagers' so often have to blow off a bit of steam before they start to think. Yearlings will make an insecure or high blooded horse very chargey around cows, and that's a hard habit to break.

Recently, I spent the afternoon ponying a show horse off a quiet mentor, gathering some good cows and calves — a wonderful opportunity for him to see that the babies, while weird and quick, are not to be feared. So many performance horses that have worked buffalo and cattle at speed in the show pen, find themselves rattled by the sheer mass of cows and calves in the pasture. By supper time, my show horse had graduated to holding his own, well on the way to becoming a confident all 'rounder.

We people are supposed to be smarter than our horses. As such, it is always our job to see that they understand what we are asking of them. The flip side, of course, is this: how can we expect our horses to understand us, when we so seldom try — I mean, really try — to understand them? This concept — which has nothing to do with burdening our horses with silly humanistic traits and schemes — will do more to help us help them, than any other one thing.

The next time we think our horse is 'bad', we must ask: when it comes to clarity, simplicity and 'do-ability', was what we requested 'good'?

I've decided, as I watch the truck and trailer lights disappear into the darkness without me, that I'm a fair-weather cowgirl and I'm fortunate that I'm allowed to feel this way. For me, happiness is not trekking out in the dark, wading through ten inches of snow, looking for cold, wet horses. Catching one, then saddling its icy back to spend the day looking for cows in the forestry. Following the snow plow down the icy highway to meet up with other like-minded individuals in this storm. Wearing horsehide mitts and leggings while handling stiff reins, jack pine boughs upside frozen faces, feet so cold you can no longer feel your toes ...

Today, I raise my cup to the rugged riders but I do not envy you. Instead, I will see you at suppertime. There will be stew.

I'm thinking a lot about being mindful these days, both with my horses and just in my own personal space. This morning, sitting in the dark comfort of the kitchen, sipping my first coffee, I challenged myself to notice something of beauty. This is an exercise in mental wellness as, God knows, I don't want to do the running, sweating kind.

What came to me was the unhurried, almost stopping, sound of a two-hundred-year-old grandfather clock standing just behind my chair. Tick. Tock. Tick. Tock. Tick. Tock.

I try to imagine what on earth this clock has seen. It never falters, never speeds up ... and unconsciously, I start breathing deeply.

This feel-good mental exercise is also useful with our horses. I will go out to them, greeting each one in turn and I thank them for bringing something beautiful to my life. I am very careful not to mention physical beauty because I think that all of us, whether women or horses, have so much more to offer than a pretty face. But I will stroke one's forelock and thank him or her for being safe and honest; another one will be thanked for being such a keen student or a much-needed dose of fun in my life ... and so on.

I don't take treats because I want them to feel the benefit of my gratitude and not be sidetracked by grub. Each horse has something beautiful they bring to the relationship and if they do not, I need to find it.

This one thing has a profound effect on how I see these horses and they, in turn, feel valued. Of course, once they have been called beautiful in some way, they try hard to make it stick. I urge you to play with this exercise that uses the power of our intentions.

Think of some common gear that prevents us from discovering and fixing problems with our horse. On a visit to a local tack store, I was dismayed to see the majority of English headstalls were sold with crank nosebands. What? I personally consider these unworthy of hanging in my (or anyone else's) tack room. How on earth does one see if the horse is soft jawed and submitting to his bit, if his mouth is winched shut? For this reason, I seldom train with a noseband, unless it's a beast with a long-ingrained problem, or else a driving horse.

Western folks need not snicker. How many of us put a breast collar on our saddles as a matter of course? What we need to do is saddle and work our horse without one for a typical ride. Does the saddle work its way back or does it stay in the right spot just behind the shoulder blade? We need to know this aspect of testing for saddle fit. Then, and only then, can we put the breast collar on our rig to equalize the pull if our horse is climbing hills, stopping and turning, galloping out or working on a rope. Otherwise, it doesn't hurt to go without. Pay attention and you'll see too many breast collars are holding saddles in the wrong spot.

Too often, the things we call helpers hinder our quest for knowledge. Whether your accessories are based on fads or tradition, do they add to your safety, as well as the comfort of your horse?

There's many a horse and pony that, as soon as you put a leg on, will 'check out of Dodge'. Often, we'll try and keep one happy by riding without any leg at all but this is counterproductive to good schooling. If the training is to progress logically, we need him to accept a system of cues that controls the larger part of his body, including his motor. If he's uptight about this contact, we have to quietly train him to relax, understand and accept.

One of the simplest ways to teach the tense horse to know and trust the leg is by working gates. Remember, just gentle slow pressure, one leg cueing, the other leg 'opening the door', like an invitation. Don't kick and please, be generous enough to stop cueing as soon as he moves a step. This slows everything down and our pony learns that stepping sideways is a good response; taking off like a jet, not so much.

When he understands, we can work on little circles, just as neat as we can make them, asking him to step over and ahead with the inside hind leg. It's a forward-sideways motion with the rear end, like turning a wheelbarrow. Work both sides and see if he'll progress to doing the exercise at trot? Finally, we'll school our downward transitions from trot (and eventually lope) to walk by pushing his inside hip up towards his eye. This exercise will keep him soft, even when he wants to resist and quicken.

So many hot horses will relax and accept the aids if we simply unbuckle our spurs and go back to using our leg. It's something riders might want to consider — especially those who wear 'em in grocery stores and restaurants.

So often, we might want our horses to go trail riding, to relax in the great outdoors. The reality is that horses unused to wind and wide-open spaces can be really hard to handle out there.

It helps to remember that once upon a time, your horse was uncertain in the arena, too. His earliest memories will be of running with his mother out in the wind and sun. It took training to make him the horse he is indoors and it will take training to get him comfortable outside again. Folks think that the trails will be fun and relaxing, so they load up and head to the mountains. Well, this might be fun for us but we forget that for many horses, trail riding is a whole other world. The good news is, any horse can be made better; the bad news is, it will take some dedication.

We start by making the arena the place for work. Hard work it is, work that demands physical and mental effort. When our horse is sweating, puffing and generally wanting to stand around, we then ride him around just outside the arena to cool him down. We don't make a point of taking another horse with us, we just stay nice and close to his comfort zone. As much as we can, we ride on a loose rein and do a lot of praise and petting.

When the horse is doing this well over several days, continue to use the arena to first ride him down. Then we'll use the great outdoors to relax and enjoy, gradually expanding our territory. If he gets silly and hot, we don't fight him; we go back indoors to work it off. Eventually, riding outside will be the restful reward we can look forward to.

Just keep gradually stretching that ol' safety zone. We like to get our horses comfortable working alone but a really awesome trail horse can be a blessing to mentor a less confident horse. Many times, particularly with geldings, they have to learn to work quietly in larger groups along the trails if they start to act dominant. If you have an 'outdoor' horse, this will all seem silly and unnecessary. For the many 'indoor' horses we come across nowadays, however, the fear of riding out is a very big deal. Remember, your horse isn't being 'bad', he lacks confidence. Fear drives each of us to act in strange ways.

Before too long, he'll look forward to going out and seeing the sights with you, his trusted friend.

REMEMBRANCE

The day is cold and snowy and as such, is perfect for telling the story of Gypsy and the toboggan. Before I give the impression that I was a naughty child, I'll have you understand that from an early age, I had some sort of a thing about driving. I was weird with it.

Games on the lawn guiding other kids by the mouths with skipping ropes had me segue into teaching my elderly Shetland to drive. She patiently laboured underneath a crusted and enormous collar, some relic of the carriage driving age, while I skidded along behind on whatever tire or piece of plywood I could find. She was safe, she was honest, she was fun ... until, in a flash, I realized there was more horsepower hanging around in the form of a bay two-year-old filly called Gypsy. I made a plan.

It was nothing to feign a grave illness and with worry on her face, my mother agreed that I should miss a day of school and stay home, in bed. O, triumph! With a roar of the engine and a cloud of exhaust, the school bus departed with my older sister at the same time as the miracle of my healing. The whereabouts of my mother remains a detail lost in the mists of time.

Within minutes, I was out of jammies and into chore clothes. I particularly remember donning red mittens knitted by my grandmother. The horses were poking about the corral, just cleaning up their morning feed. Gypsy had been handled enough that it was no big deal getting her caught and tied, but putting the harness on was another matter.

Eventually, I got her snubbed short to a fence post and by hanging off the top rail, forced her to take the bit. I knew that I'd have to leave her tied if I was ever going to manage threading the lines back through the terrets and hook up the aluminum toboggan without getting kicked. Still, she danced around enough to make it difficult. I was all of eight years old.

When the moment of reckoning arrived, I unsnapped the rope from her halter, grabbed the cold-kinked lines in my mittened hands and threw myself on the toboggan. The two-year-old was rooted to the spot. "Gypsy, gittup!" I yelled and slapped the lines on her rump. It was the last thing I really remember.

When I sat up, I was halfway down the lane with no pony or toboggan in sight. Behind me lay the red mittens like little dead birds. A neighbour spotted the bay headed east, going hard, the silver toboggan sailing out behind like a shingle on the wind. He had the presence of mind to jump into his truck and keep her in sight. When a new barbed wire fence eventually brought her down, by kneeling on Gypsy's neck, he was able to wait for help to arrive.

Meanwhile, back at the barn, I began to worry. My father was a bit of a disciplinarian and there was something about how the day was unfolding that was beginning to bother me. While the neighbour had kindly returned the wild-eyed pony, mended the three fences she'd torn out and fetched what was left of our harness, including one flattened toboggan, I prayed he wouldn't feel the need to tell my dad.

He did, of course, and in the end, I was right to be concerned. Sitting was a careful process for quite a while afterward and in time, the toboggan and harness were duly repaired. Within the year, Gypsy would be taught to drive by hands more experienced than mine ... and while the leggy bay pony went on to serve honourably for many years, to her dying day, she was always hard to hook up.

1976. The year my riding changed for the better.

I was twelve when my mother wisely realized that if I was to improve, we needed to up the ante. Enter Friar Tuck, a seventeen-year-old Dartmoor-Thoroughbred cross who had the distinction of beating the celebrated Dresden to go champion at Devon. He was an AHSA High-Score (now called Pony Finals) contender in the Larges for many years.

Friar Tuck had just been brought into Canada by Lady Gordon and it was rumoured he might be available to lease for the year.

Long story short, he was and we did it. My time with Tuck became one of the pivotal points in my life. This bold, fiercely competitive pony was a guiding light. I have only a few grainy and faded snapshots of the time Tuck and I spent together but I remember what he had to teach me like it was yesterday. The bottom line? If you can lease and learn from Incredible, don't be too quick to buy Second Best.

Had an interesting time at the posh vet clinic yesterday. There was I, standing holding the grotty lead rope of Brown Betty, surrounded by $80,000 horses, when the veterinarian called us into the consultation room and asked what it was that my beast did for a living. We were surrounded by 8x10 glossies of their most famous patients — working cowhorse, cutting and open jumper champions — and I could only think to say, "She's just a kids' pony."

"All right," he barked to the assistant. "Look sharp here. We've got a horse with a very important job!" I could've hugged him on the spot.

I write this in memory of E.M. Boerschmann. Hard taskmaster, miserly in her praise, the nearly five years spent with her were pivotal. Decades on, her wisdom is still my compass.

At the time I was riding under this brilliant, older woman, I did not understand her scorn of modern dressage competition and mankind's hardwired need to win. I did not understand why our quiet hours spent schooling were never to be justified with prizes or appreciative judges, all the trappings I associated with real dressage.

Once, at age sixteen, I snuck away with my mother and our lovely horse to the Provincial Dressage Championships to ride at what is now Third Level — because I needed something to show for all my hard work. Despite tying with a well-known rider for the win, my teacher was disgusted at my betrayal. It was a lesson that riding well should be why we're riding. Improving the horse is the reward.

Her teaching taught me to look beyond names, trophies and gifted movers. To this day, I wince when even a photograph or piece of art portrays the horse as ridden incorrectly. Instead, I keep in my memory the image of the classically trained horse: one showing the beauty of what is achieved without tension, side reins, snug cavessons, or force.

Please note, going from back to front because this is how it must happen … the deep step under of the carrying hind leg … the upward arch of the lumbar directly behind the saddle … the lack of any tension in the tail … the uphill feel to the canter … the lack of hollowing or wrinkling in front of the withers … the lack of any tension or discernible muscling along the neck … the lack of a 'broken' crest (as seen by a notable bend midway) … the lack of a convex bulge underneath the neck … the bridle crown as the horse's highest point.

Note the lack of tension and a levelness in the ears, eyes and jaws of the horse … the comfortably slack noseband to allow the softly champing mouth … the lack of tension in the rider's face or hands … the straight line between the rider's bent elbow and the horse's bit … the horse's face never behind the vertical … NEVER behind the vertical, no matter the judges, no matter the sport … and finally, the shared joy and effortless flow of energy between the rider and the horse.

Forwards, backwards, sideways, always — this must be our goal. How does it happen? The horse is asked to stretch and then, the rider gently takes it back again. Ad infinitum. Is it easy? Never, though paradoxically, it shouldn't be hard. No matter the level of his training, the horse is stretched and gently gathered to start the session, then every few minutes thereafter. The horse's walk, his enjoyment and the shaping of his body tell us if our work is good.

This standard of dressage training has been the golden mean for more than two hundred years. In respect to my teacher and the effort that went into just one word of "Gut!" from her, I am speaking up. Note that it is not the idea of competition that offends me but, rather, when the ideals of correct riding are ignored.

I'm old enough to remember when horse show prizes, sumptuous trays and trophy cups, were made of silver or brass. The more you won, the more you polished. Dating myself further, I also miss the gala shows: all breeds and disciplines, live organ music, banks of flowers, the roving spot light, an audience turned out in evening dress. Nowadays, breed shows have taken over. We don't mix much anymore.

I miss the show hacks. A far cry from today's hunters under saddle, these horses were gay and lively, beautifully presented, checkerboards on their rumps, bits and bradoons clinking softly, all eyes sparkling in anticipation of "Extend the

Trot!" It was a class for the classically trained horses. Their soft steps in collected canter, riders elegant in tail coats and top hats, is something I'll never forget.

Something to think about today. We hear so many complaints about the inconvenience of old age. Instead, please think of those people who were never given the chance to grow old. When I was a child, I memorized this saying, embroidered by my grandmother:

> "Let me grow lovely, growing old, so many old things do.
> Laces and ivory and gold and silks need not be new.
> There is healing in old trees, old streets, a glamour hold.
> Why not I, as well as they, grow lovely, growing old?"

We love the idea of honourable retirement for the old campaigner, turning him out as "he doesn't owe us a thing". But when this dear soul is ready to cash in his chips, what then? We try not to see it: the skin-and-bones horse that cannot chew, the grey-muzzled dog that cannot rise, the cancer-eye cow with "one more calf in her". What then?

This week, it's minus twenty and worse in Alberta. There is far more to come. That old horse was a good one; he'll have green grass in Paradise from here on in. He gave of his best twenty years ago, a storybook win that made you. He was the greatest horse ever. Please, tell him you love him. It's time to say goodbye.

Bloody horses. A phone call: I've a horse out on the road, heading south. Again. (Oh, Lord, how many horses do I need to kill on the highway?) Cody, having finished his grain in the yard, has gone walkabout. Straight for the blacktop, he takes the turn, then resolutely jogs smack down the yellow line.

A lifetime later, or maybe three minutes, I'm following him with the horse trailer, hazards flashing. Eventually Cody stops and goes, "Hey, can I hitch a ride?" He sticks his nose in the halter, I open the trailer door and he gets on. Slam. In front of a highly-amused audience of two big rigs and a school bus,

I might add. Me in my purple basset hound jammies 'cause I've just come in from riding and am wet and cold.

Gotta love relief, served up with a heapin' side of humiliation. Then, we head home.

I've just found my old charm bracelet.

Those of a certain age will remember. One Christmas morning, a sterling silver bracelet would be in the toe of your stocking. Rich with the promise of summer vacations, souvenirs, graduations and other rites of passage ... it was telling you to get on with your life.

The goal, of course, was to have a bracelet loaded with beautiful memories. I'd moved on to other pursuits before mine was properly filled. Looking back, charm bracelets had gone out of style — much like station wagon road trips and 'sweet sixteens' had, as well.

Nevertheless, I stuck with collecting long enough to amass eight charms. Right now, there's a smile on my weathered face, remembering each of them.

One charm means more to me than the others. Given to me by a neighbour, it's a skilfully-made pony and cart.

As a kid, school did not come easily. I was smart enough but I never seemed able to find my crowd. Teachers often hectored me, despite my shyness and good behaviour. I was brutalized by an older boy every day after school at our rural bus stop. To make matters worse, I was unwell, absent often enough that firm friendships were forged without me.

By the time I'd made it to junior high, school life was well-nigh intolerable. Nothing was right in my life ... but I had horses.

My favourite was a small palomino gelding called Sovereign. Sovy, a purebred Welsh pony, had been given to me to train — which was miracle enough — by an elderly lady in the area. From the 1940s to the '60s, she'd owned a high-class Shetland show barn.

Soon after Sovy's arrival, trunks of Freedman harness, embroidered blankets and other costly accoutrements arrived at our door, a maroon viceroy and gaily-pinstriped roadster bike among them. I still can hardly imagine it.

Sovy turned out to be the perfect student for an intense child. My mistakes were absorbed without judgment and my enthusiasms were bravely carried to the fore. Ground driving segued seamlessly into touring with the roadster bike. Ears up, wheels flashing, we were familiar sights on every road within miles of our little white-fenced farm.

Eventually, Sovy and I made it to the show ring. We were bedazzled by the roving spot light, live organ music and evening dress of the Calgary International Horse Show. As a four-year-old trained by a twelve-year-old kid, he managed to place a respectable third in the Children's Driving. It was a lofty achievement for the young pony and his awkward girl.

Sovy's biggest gifts, however, were the miles he carried me far from my troubles, trotting along while the wind dried my tears.

One day a neighbour, Mrs. Lyons, waved us to a stop at the end of her lane. "I want you to know how much enjoyment I get from watching you and your pony," she said, pressing a little blue Birks box into my hand. I was surprised by her kind gesture. I hope I remembered to thank her.

At home, the box was opened and there was the little pony and cart. I treasured it but as the years passed, it was set aside, just as I went on without Sovereign.

I remember the sound of his shoes on the hardtop, the supple feel of those beautiful lines in my hands. To think that I took this for granted. I clip the tarnished bracelet around my wrist, start to sniffle and feel the need to blink.

I was fifteen years old and schooling Eclipse on lead changes with my German teacher. Her advice was good then; it's still good now. Here's an excerpt from my riding diary, dated May, 1979.

"By going at a strong canter and ridden really roundly, their hind legs are naturally under them and pistoning. Mrs. Boerschmann says this is more than half the battle for a clean lead change. When he trades 'I think I can' for 'I know I can', then he can be allowed to slow down, so long as he keeps moving forward. Eclipse wants to slow down, so this will not be hard to accomplish.

"Do not use the whip or spur for a lead change. It will only speed up the horse and make him associate the change with discomfort. Sometimes when a horse gets upset during lead changes, it helps to teach them from the counter canter. Turn the natural lead into a counter canter by crossing on the diagonal and picking up the new circle with the same leg. Before the horse gets really tired — but just tired enough for incentive — I'll stay on the twenty-metre circle and quietly change my legs. Usually, he'll change legs too and the reward — the relief — is the lead change.

"For now, we're riding demi-voltes and changing a stride before we get back to the wall. One way — our left to right — is better than the other.

"Hot horses can learn to look forward to changing leads by quietly being asked to walk immediately afterwards. Push-ride horses can be encouraged after a change by being given a very long rein immediately after, while continuing their canter, always with much praise and stroking.

"Mrs. B says I need to learn to quit while I'm ahead."

My small pony harness is very old, very dear to me and this year, for the first time, I'm feeling as though I've outlived its usefulness. I brought it tenderly into the house from the tack shed today, preparing to clean and condition it, keeping it safe for the winter on its cast iron hook in the house.

The set belonged to a mentor and was made sometime before the second world war. The faint logo still visible on the bridle tells us that in its day, it was the very best quality that money could buy. Polished and buffed to a turn, it still would hold up to the closest scrutiny in presentation. I was always proud of the ponies it had helped to various championships, long before I was around to hold the reins.

So, there it is ... glowing with the vibration of good horsemanship and stunning animals, cheering crowds and victory. It has been a charmed thing, bringing me nothing but joy. I dig around in a tuft of the back pad and find a few white hairs, memento of the best pony I know I will ever drive. He is now 28 years old.

I smile over a beautiful mend where the crupper D in the back pad pulled out of the tree one day, less than a week before a hugely important event — or, so it seemed to me at the time. The generosity of the original maker's grandson in Toronto, along with a kind courier driver, made sure that the repaired piece was ready for the competition. On the wall of our tack room hangs the picture where the harness, the pony and I were all, for one brief instant, at the very top of our game.

For many years, the smoothly worn brass rings in the back pad were changed out with tandem terrets and I'm thinking of these — where on earth are they? — and of the cracking pair of chestnut mares who went through life with their hair straight back and of course, sitting tall behind them, so did I.

The breeching straps were the first to show wear and in time, these were replaced, as were the reins, along with the delicate rolled leather adorning the bridle. Then the breast collar began looking weary and made way for a patent show collar — another piece from another mentor — along with elegant brass hames. The Liverpool bit was worn by the brilliant Peter, a childhood favourite who died when I was in grade five. I'm thinking of him now as I check the hinges for wear. And yes, even the old bit is looking tired.

I'm remembering all this as I'm cleaning, realizing that all good things must come to an end. This set hung idle for close to a decade, years I struggled with illness and change, until this fall when it came out and graced Tom Jones on a special day. It was always lucky and never once involved in a wreck. I have driven untold hours and miles with this harness, knowing by heart just how it smells and how the tug buckles jingle. The leather, three quarters of a century on, is still fine grained, buttery soft yet firm.

But it is time.

When it's time to say goodbye ...

I very recently made the heartrending decision to euthanize two young ponies; the first, due to a physical issue that was growing unmanageable and the second, with a mental or emotional issue that had him savaging others in the herd, horses he'd been friends with for years. In both cases, these gentle souls were becoming strangers to me. It was only a matter of time before someone — man or beast — got hurt.

Such decisions are painful. Have I overlooked something hugely wrong in my training? Have I rushed them, or demanded too much? Have I waited long enough to find a miracle? Do they just need another chance? Am I the worst sort of flake or a failure? Oh, to not be one more human being who lets them down.

For me, personally, when anyone or anything starts causing my sleepless nights, when the possibility of injury becomes probability, it's time to go to that place where none of us wants to go.

Mixed in with my love of these beautiful animals is Ego, saying that if I try hard enough, long enough, I can fix them. Well, I was wrong.

When I was a kid, English riding was a foreign concept in my neck of the woods. Wanting to do so simply meant that you were weird. Our model of perfection was the British Horse Society's old *"Manual of Horsemanship"* and we did our best, despite barbed wire fences and the lack of an actual Pony Club, to follow this book to a tee. One thing that strikes me as I scroll by today's ads for tack and ergonomic riding clothes, is how styles have changed within my lifetime.

First of all, helmets were a bit of a fluid notion. People often jumped at play days in either flat cloth caps or bowlers, even with bare heads. I vividly remember the day that the Canadian Equestrian Federation steward started enforcing the rule that our velvet hunt caps required chin straps of some kind. Oh, the scramble to fashion such back at the trailer, so that we might still be able to jump and compete.

Our elephant ear jodhs and breeks were bulletproof, made of whipcord with a dozen teeny little buttons to struggle with. When Harry Hall came out with two-way stretch fabric, suddenly, a whole new world opened up to us, a world of rust and startling canary.

We wore ratcatcher shirts with matching chokers or complicated stocks that needed correct tying, along with a pin that was to be a plain little hunting whip, nothing more. On chilly days, we showed in beautiful hourglass-cut tweed coats — whether or not we were hourglass-shaped — of an elegant length that covered one's derriere. Hot days, we brought out our cream or baby blue linens. Gloves were always brown.

Boots were a whole different story. There were no zippers, kids, and if they were easy to put on, they didn't fit. Oh, the desperate moments before one's class, trying to fit boot pulls, baby powder, even Saran Wrap all inside the boots, without rucking up the breeks.

Patent boot tops were all the rage when I was young and I was never lucky enough to have them, but my sister did. Spurs sat high upon the counter seam of one's dress boots; any lower, they were wrong. Our boots were also much shorter than we see now, built of a stiffer leather. Dehner and Vogel were the ones. I have mine, still.

Now, depending on how old and traditional your teacher was — mine were all crusty pre-war types — you might have a sheepskin under your saddle, or no pad at all. The saddles were flocked with wool and would more or less pack down to the horse's shape. Hermes close contact saddles were the new thing, with their cutback heads and absolutely nothing in front of, underneath or behind your leg.

A huge game changer was the addition of rubber treads in the stirrup irons. We used flat bridles for showing with plain snaffles, or full bridles or pelhams — and the latter two had rolled leather lip straps as well as curb chains. Children were expected to understand and be proficient with double reins at an early age and they were. Black tack was considered cheap and classless, even in dressage, so all tack was brown — and no sparkles on your browband. Actually, no sparkles, period. Whether saddlery, clothing or teachers, all the best came straight from England.

When showing, we usually had to drop our stirrups for equitation classes and these had to be crossed in front of the saddle to rest on the horse's shoulders. No swinging, dangling irons. Judges thought nothing of asking us to switch and ride one another's horses.

For really important days we braided 'buttons' down the neck with thread. Ordinary days got yarn. Tails were pulled to lie flat along the dock, with checkerboards on the rumps of hacks. We trotted and cantered 'round to live organ music, all in the quest to earn trophies that one had to actually polish. Oh, those beautiful silver cups and trays from way back, when I was a kid ...

Western. I can close my eyes and still see the colours in the ring, without a sparkly crystal in sight. Hats, chaps and Tony Lama boots were all matching. You could find every colour under the sun. I remember when one-piece 'equitation suits' first came in — woe betide anyone lacking the body of a gymnast. These were made-to-measure in stretchy fortrel fabric, with elaborate yokes, cuffed sleeves and belt loops that sat just above our matching hipster, slightly bell-bottomed chaps.

Boots, if you were on trend, had sharp toes with buck stitching and iguana toe caps. We all wore our hair in large buns pinned under our high crown hats, unless we wore 'bunches' gathered at each jaw, tied with long-tailed bows of thick, matching yarn. Our narrow scarves were fastened at our throats with beautiful Birks silver pins. Looking back, it was a strange blend of Old Californios mixed with American Bandstand.

Boys were more workmanlike in white starched dress shirts with either tailored vests and ties, or in hot weather, with short folded scarves tied in square granny knots. Over their plaid hopsack Wranglers, they wore their shotguns in earthy colours, unlike the rest of us. My someday husband was out there on his dynamite palomino, way out of my league as he was four years older. Meanwhile, there was I, chubby and freckle-faced, chuffing along in the Under 12:2s.

Picture real silver bridles — really beautiful bridles, Victors and the like — with almost everyone using romal reins. Navajo saddle blankets sometimes came with a matching fringe over the quarters, which you'd promptly cut off once you saw how rough-looking these made your horse. Our saddles often had silver laced cantles with engraved name plates, buckstitched skirts and sterling conchos. You hardly ever saw a breast collar.

At the recognized shows, we were all required to carry hobbles, braided riatas and slickers of a colour to match our chaps. Rolling a show slicker neatly was a bit of an art. For cold weather, does anyone remember those old Woods and Sprung down-filled winter jackets? Again, such beautiful colours, nipped in at the waist and with contrasting fuzzy collars. Everybody-who-wanted-to-be-somebody wore one.

I still consider this era's western pleasure horses the epitome of elegance. Bridled up, they really walked, jogged and loped out, going straight with the rail and not canted in. I remember that there was quite an art to tapering their tails just below the hocks with a jack knife.

Again, we'd be prepared to swap horses in Stock Seat and only the final six or so were expected to ride patterns after showing first on the rail. Mounting and dismounting were also a regular part of judging horsemanship and there was many a time I rued my skin-tight show chaps.

I'll remember the sound of lined up horses contentedly rolling their crickets 'til my dying day.

I learned, early on, the value in honest-to-goodness, everyday work. Not schooling, necessarily, not finding fault, but the calming, character-building stuff of just showing up in all sorts of weather and doing a job. It might look easy, but building a relationship with a pony until he is standing on his own, waiting for me to fill the stone boat, then walking out to a different spot in the stubble field to fork it off and come back again, is huge. Back and forth, day in, day out, just doing something well.

After the passing of a winter, it's but a small step to the rock-solid pony, the best harness, the presentation carriage, the lovely hat. In the end, it's an old-fashioned but thorough way to train a reliable pony or horse.

Thus, a day in the lives of my driving ponies — even the ones who ruled the show ring for many years. Looking back, I was blessed to have handled both their pitchforks — and their reins.

As a hushed arena on a sunny morning brings to mind a cathedral, there is so much emotion that lives in a tack room full of well-loved things. I am thinking of this as I straighten a pair of reins, hang up some spurs that were kicked off in a hurry, sweeping out a forgotten corner.

Tack rooms can take us for a ride down memory lane.

I have several such spots that go by the moniker: the first, out in the shed for the workaday stuff; the second, my organized mayhem that lives in the trailer; the third, the tack room here in the house. When the kids grew up and left home, I turned the boys' room into a place where it could all live together, the books, old pictures and prizes, along with all the gear.

Gracing it all, of course, is my old wing chair for slow-starting mornings and late-night reads. This chair, more accurately, belongs to the cats.

"Way to erase any sign of us!" said the boys. Not so. Did they not know that I made this room so that I could remember? I kept their old cowboy wallpaper and the curtain rod made from a branding iron. On the floor sprawls a hide rug harvested from a bovine character who once grazed these hills.

Saddle racks, eight in all, hang from the walls. This keeps the floor clear, for easy sweeping. A few of these racks hold a rotating collection of sidesaddles — some of which I use, others, here only to be repaired and sent on. The others are carrying stock saddles that bring to mind the different horses who packed them.

One of these is a neat little rig from the 1940s. It is just the right size for a 13:3 paint pony and a wiry pre-teen boy. The stirrups hang turned, as though the saddle's waiting. I see teeth marks where a bored horse scraped the front fork while tied alongside it at the hitching rail. I smile, remembering in turn the boy, the bored horse and the beautiful paint pony. It's hard to believe it's been years since they last rode.

A row of bridles marches across three of the walls. Perhaps the most nostalgic of these is the plainest. A functional one ear headstall with its original Crockett bit, chin strap and split reins, given to me on my eleventh birthday. It bears evidence of much use. Crooked, homemade holes show how my horses and I grew in size. It came from the old Macleod's Hardware Store, now long gone.

Another bridle, beautiful but tiny, used on their ponies by our children when they were small. If I look closely, I can still see the bends where we'd tie the reins into an 'ice cream cone' so that they couldn't be dropped while the kids rode. My husband's spurs from when he was a boy. My favourite horse stories while growing up. Black and white photos from another time: my sidesaddle mentor; horse show victories; the beautiful Eclipse; my daughter as a toddler; Piper under a trophy cooler larger than himself.

I straighten the whips. One, a gift of sorts, from my dressage teacher — I can still remember her exasperation when she pointed out that my right leg was woefully weak. "There. No more excuses!" she proclaimed in her thick, German accent as she pressed the long whip into my hand. Another, a beautiful antique from the horse and carriage era, hangs from the whip reel on the wall. It was bent over like a shepherd's hook when I bought it at an auction, long ago. I smile when I think of steaming the holly rod straight over a boiling pot of soup and how, with care, it again was a beautiful thing.

A row of old riding diaries on a shelf of books. I used to gnash my teeth at being made to keep them. Now, of course, they are among my treasures. I pull one out and idly riffle through it: golden truths, hastily drawn diagrams, teenage angst and woes.

There is the set of harness that graced some of the best driving ponies imaginable. I recently retired it, newly cleaned and polished, mere days after Piper, the last to wear it, had died. Unknowingly I did this but somehow, still, I knew that it was an era ended. Beside this old, beloved set hangs a brand-new single harness. It silently mocks me, "C'mon, Lee, time's a wastin'. What are you waiting for?" I turn away, wondering if it wants to be sold.

Boots, custom made, that will never again fit me unless I'm held captive, without food, for a year. Bridles favoured by certain horses and then, not liked by any, ever again. A few silver bits that, if I'm honest, I fancied much more than my horses did. Some things, I see that I'm keeping, because they are my last link to a life that has vanished. Others, I'm keeping because of fond hopes and dreams.

I finish my sweeping. Smiling, I turn out the light and gently close the door.

'TIS THE SEASON

Thinking of a pony for Christmas?

It's a lovely notion, but whoa there. Adding a new member to the herd can be stressful at the best of times, never mind the exhausting holiday schedule and bitterly cold weather. For your new pony to really fit into your life, take the time to shop carefully, have a few trial rides — and plan for a round of lessons or ongoing saddle time to start the process of getting to know one another.

When we buy a pony in the deepest, darkest winter, we're often forced to turn him out and wait several months until the ground is conducive to riding again. That's not the best way to start a relationship, especially when children are involved.

Rather than bring a new pony home for the holidays, why not put a card on the tree, promising to start pony shopping over the coming months? Oh, the excitement of looking forward to something after the holidays. Better yet, give your child the gift of riding lessons this winter with an excellent local teacher who can fuel the fires and teach her how to care for and handle a pony of her own. These are just two ways to encourage good horsemanship and celebrate the gift of giving — without the stress of a looming deadline.

If you're thinking of a pony for Christmas, hold your horses. Avoid the hasty decision that, for safety's sake, so often needs to be undone.

You've bought your dream horse and suddenly, the wheels have fallen off. What's gone wrong? He's spooky, he won't go soft and round, he's hard to catch and now, he's pulling back when tied. Don't panic. There's a chance you've bought the wrong horse — but there's a bigger chance Mr. Right is homesick.

Stay in touch with his last owner or take some lessons with the former trainer, if you can. Stick with his old feed schedule and the same amount of turn-out time. Double check that you're using the same type of bit and do your best, for the next while, to replicate his old riding program. You won't always have to do it this way.

When you brought home your dream horse, you suddenly rocked his world. He has found himself in a strange land with strange customs. His friends are gone and you're in his space, a complete stranger who wants to bond. He's the new kid in town and the new herd wants nothing to do with him.

If this horse was a child, you'd know instinctively that he was homesick, that he was upset and yelling he wants to go home. While he's in mourning, please don't bribe him or try to remake him. Be safe, be fair, be constant. Give him lots of opportunity to work off his troubles. In time — six days? six weeks? six months? — if he was a good horse before, he will probably come around.

Remember, a horse's level of homesickness has little to do with the level to which he is trained.

A cold snap. The horses, ranging and browsing along far hills, turn tail to the wind and deny any comforts to be found at the corrals. Until one day in winter, when I peer out the frosted glass and see him, standing alone at the big gate to the yard. It is time, he is telling me. Time to come in and don the warm rug and start on winter's feed.

This ritual of the old horse waiting, me calling his name, the low nicker in thanks will be a daily thing until one seemingly ordinary day, sometime in May — a day that smells of the wakening earth, when he says he has made it through another one and no longer needs my help.

This wisdom that lives in old horses is something that, if we are witness to it, makes us feel blessed.

Some people get it and some people don't. Turn out is that indefinable thing that lets you know you are in the presence of somebody's passion. While the traditional disciplines such as showing hunters or carriage driving are rife with rules of what not to do or wear, the notion of turn out goes far beyond the show ring.

Rain gloves tucked under seat cushions, plaited manes done just so, bits and hardware all gleaming — but what about the other things? The state of your horse's shoeing, the halter hanging up neatly back at the trailer, leg wraps rolled for the trip home, water buckets washed, the trailer cleaned out between hauls. Being tidy has little to do with money.

Take pride, not because someone is judging, but because horses are our passion. They deserve our very best.

"Our breath is the bridge that unites body and mind." — Thich Nhat Hanh.

Whether starting colts or 'entering at A', remember to breathe. I love this simple wisdom from the Buddhist monk. Mindfulness is a worthy goal, whoever we are, wherever our steps may lead.

One of the misunderstood aspects of modern horsemanship is this united, happy partnership thing. While this is a high ideal, we can easily lose sight of the fact that once our equals, few horses are happy lowering themselves to being common labourers again. It's a boundaries issue that seems to underlie all healthy relationships — whether with our animals or co-workers, even our own friends.

I could describe my horse relationships best by saying that I want my horses to be on 'company manners' around me. You know how it is when you're a house guest with someone you don't want to offend? You value the relationship, so you're constantly considering your part in the deal. Do you take your shoes off inside the door? Pour your own coffee? Do the dishes? Are you staying up too late or sleeping in? See where I'm going with this? You want to be invited back and so, you'll not be playing loud music, using all the hot water or the last of the milk.

This is how I want my horses and I to commune: in mutual respect, with a desire to please one another and comfortably fit in. Always, always, however, I want them to be gracious guests in my life, easy to get along with because they do not want to offend. Safety aside, it's ultimately the kindest thing.

I went to a horse sale yesterday and it was fun, wearing my town togs, seeing old friends, lunching on coffee and french fries. I grew up begging to go to horse sales and even now, I wandered the pens, imagining the possibilities found in every single young horse.

What wasn't fun was watching so many broke old-timers, into their late teens and twenties, being ridden through the ring. Ears up and chins tucked, they were still doing their jobs with pride, showing their neck reining and obedience. One final act of service, bringing in one last cheque. It was wrenching enough, the ones bringing a decent dollar but we all knew where those were headed that were fetching two hundred bucks.

This is not a comment on the meat industry and what we do with all the inferior animals that are bred and put on the market. No. It is, however, a call to those with horses who have long served and are done. Trust me, there are good people who would love to be mentored by such horses but if it's gone beyond that, as it eventually does, please allow them to die at home.

Maybe this bothers me more than it should but I will say that hypocrisy is a heavy burden, especially in the long dark hours before dawn. I've been guilty of shipping the loyal, high-mileage horses, of finding closure in pocketing that one final cheque.

I've tried consoling myself with believing that things were different back then — that horses were livestock, there were no free rides, the winters were brutal and one obeyed Those Who Knew Best. The cost to me has been in remembrance of backing up to the chutes among liner loads of unwanted horses and standing, bent double with anguish, as old friends clip-clopped trustingly down the alleyway, a glimpse of my little son's face as he watched from the truck.

For those who say that life is hard, that money's money and that it's only business, I say be careful. These decisions we make, or that we allow ourselves to be talked into, have a habit of sneaking up on us in the quiet hours. They tap us on the shoulder and no, we do not forget.

Mike and I have lived both sides of this. For years, it's been considered shoddy stockmanship to send a working horse that has given his best on to unknown hands. We've all given tired out horses to 'forever' homes, only to find that they've either been sold on at auction or put back into demanding work. Because the bottom line seemed always tight, some of the working horses would be put down but many were sent on at so many cents a pound.

Hard, yes, but until modern times, horses were considered livestock and lived very hard lives. I always understood this but still, it was something that did not settle easily with my own personal truth.

A few years ago, I was put on the other side of the fence when, after a shattering illness and loss of bravado, I was given the gift of one of these high mileage, honest old horses. He proceeded to change my life. I like to think that these last years with me have also added something to his.

In the end, what others think has little bearing on a matter that makes me my own harshest judge. I urge all horse owners to draw up written plans for their animals, should something happen that has others calling the shots on the horses they love.

It interests me that good horse people are so often dog or cat people, as well. It would seem that an affinity for all animals is keyed in with a feeling for horses. Consequently, I have never completely felt at ease with people who show no love for animals. Nor do I find it easy to trust those not made welcome by my dog.

Is your horse happy about you handling his legs and feet? If he's antsy about you touching them, there's usually a reason. Make sure you have a verbal or tactile cue to pick up the feet. This might be a squeeze of the hand on the back tendon or else the word, "Foot!" Otherwise, how does he know when you want to brush his legs or clip them without him moving a hair? A pony that doesn't like his lower legs touched can be helped by gently rubbing the cannon bones with a grooming mitt. This often-neglected part of the pony gets flaky and itchy and he'll quickly learn to appreciate the relief.

Likewise, be mindful how you release the foot when you are finished handling it. Too often, people — and this includes our friends the farriers — drop the foot when they are done with it. This can lead to tension on the part of the pony. Far better to quietly set the foot down when you are done. Your pony will thank you and you will have a more trusting and chilled partner.

In our experience, farriers will graciously set the feet down if politely asked. A flat-out refusal to do so would have us looking for another farrier.

Jumping for joy? Alas, I gave up on that dream eons ago.

One of my most shameful secrets stems from a long ago wreck I had while jumping with Montcalm. He'd caught his front end and cartwheeled into the ground. I landed underneath him, of course, and by the time I was well enough to try it again, I'd been accepted as a fulltime student under the German dressage teacher who would forever change me. I've never jumped again.

Riding with her was a wonderful opportunity but it had its drawbacks. Instead of dusting myself off and getting back in the game, I had decades to replay the accident over and over. The upshot is, I've lost my courage.

I was thinking about this last night — in the darkness, clutching my little blankie — after reading a message from a follower who'd read one of my posts and said, "My God, you're brave." Well, I'm not because I've got things that I'm scared of, too.

Jumping is the big one. I also know it will be a frosty Friday before I ever get behind a team of fresh Percherons on a hayrack, which is a whole other story. Let's just say I've never before seen bit shanks bent backwards after someone's been trying to stop a runaway, have you?

Truth is, we all have our little somethings. If we have a certain amount of intelligence and imagination, our nerves can get the better of us. I know that someday I will want to get over my jumping roadblock, if ever I have the pleasure of riding a Steady Eddie and hiring a teacher I can trust.

Just know that once we've walked this earth a while, we all have our vulnerabilities. No one is immune to them and sometimes, these hurts make us more compassionate trainers and smarter riders. What I've learned is that the power of shame dissipates the minute we talk about it and bring it to light.

How long does it take to train a pony to drive? I'm asked this often and my answer is always, "It depends".

It depends on how reliable you want your driving pony. It depends on your pony's character and prior experiences, bad and good. It depends on how handy you are as a whip.

You see, there is no pat answer. What I will say is please, please, please never make the mistake of assuming it is safer to drive your pony than it is to ride her, because it is not. All I know for sure is the older I get, the more deliberately I school through the basics. Simply put, until my pony has mastered one step, we do not move on to the next.

Buying a horse is difficult. I get that. Not only do you have a sudden change in your bank account, but the whole place seems to be in an uproar. The quiet horse you purchased last week is actually pretty lively; the quiet horses you already own are on the rampage. Before you know it, doubt starts seeping in. So, what can you do to help?

Get riding. Find a teacher if you're not confident on your own and start hauling to regular lessons, at least once per week. More often, if you can swing it. Will you and your horse ever gel? Yes! We've found, however, that letting one 'settle in' can be counter-productive. The best way to make your new horse a part of your life is to simply begin.

Allowing our pony to graze whenever he feels like it is akin to raising an ill-mannered child. He may be decent and smart but his need for instant gratification makes him hard to love. When a pony is with me, either haltered or with his bridle on, he does not eat grass unless invited to do so. In my mind, the ability to stand quietly without eating is a highly-underrated skill.

By the way, when we train, even the spoiled or formerly mishandled ones, hand-fed treats are not on our agenda. We seldom give food rewards — except to our loyal band of retirees. As our trusted associates, working ponies are not insulted with bribes. They are expected to do their best, and when they do, they are praised with heartfelt thanks and a rest. Our goal is creating partners that are happy just pleasing us. To me, the best part in knowing horses is that their friendship is earned, not bought.

That said, food rewards do have their place in training exceptionally tense horses and ponies, as moving their jaws invites relaxation. The wisdom is in knowing all the whys and the wheres and the whens.

So many riders are working to keep their horses 'in frame' with their hands. This doesn't work, folks, because the minute we let up on the pressure, the horse leaks out the cracks. Instead, we must teach our horse that when he gives us a soft feel, we too, will soften. It's not rocket science. Giving a reward when someone does the right thing means we don't need to throw slack, we just need to have feeling.

No matter our discipline, we require only a giving spirit and a willingness to lighten up. Try it; you'll like it. This could be your best year, yet.

One of our goals should be to train, while somehow encouraging the horse or pony to retain her pride. These days, we see so many going along in a mechanical or downtrodden fashion... and why wouldn't they? These trudging souls are deemed the winners in all too many horse sports.

We're often asked how to control 'the liveliness' when riding out of doors. It makes me wonder: have so few people ever ridden a joyful horse? Even sadder, who are we to deny their good feelings? Nobody wants to ride one that might buck or bolt but a little snort or a gandy-dance shouldn't be cause for alarm.

To stay safe during the winter or the time of green grass fever — no hot feed, give lots of turnout time and even a few laps with the lunge line or the round pen — but please, don't drill out all her fun.

This month is rich in memories. I remember:

Days spent singing — and well, eating a fair bit, if I'm honest — with my old friends, getting ourselves into some sort of shape for the annual Christmas concert. We'd keep telling people that we were doing old favourites by popular demand but everyone knew that we'd been too lazy to learn anything new ...

One Christmas Eve when truck and trailer lights shone down the lane, heralding the arrival of Cody, a gift from our soon-to-be son-in-law. Or memories of setting up Uncle Jack's antique train set and how, as it circled the tree, Mike and Kitty would jostle for a good seat up front. He, to blow the tin whistle each time the train passed; the old calico cat, just to gaze in wonder ...

Hanging the lovely angel from the chandelier, the one with the really big feet ... Thinking of the year that our house was so small and cramped that the toddler, sitting in her high chair, pulled the Christmas tree into the gravy on the stove and started a fire ... The real pine boughs nailed below every window, old musical instruments nestled among them and Rocky, the antique skin horse, watching another blessed season go by ...

Singalongs with unpracticed fingers on the un-tuned piano and how nobody ever knows the words to God Rest Ye, Merry Gentlemen but we sing loudly, nonetheless... The reality of constant mess and the fact that despite vowing otherwise, you've gone ahead and gained seven pounds... Being invited out, taking gingerbread men as hostess presents and watching even the stuffiest of dinner guests dissolve into laughter as we bite off their heads ...

Donning pearls and velvet and our warmest chore boots to attend the lovely country church of St. Aidan's. The rising smell of the barnyard as we warm up, the neighbour lady pumping away at the wheezy old organ, while we protect our candles from draughts and all-together-now sing, Silent Night ...

Pulling out box after box from the creepy attic, finding a spot on the mantle for the 1930s chalkware nativity scene, reuniting the main players with their broken off heads. I love the way the wisest of the wise men always looks as though he needs a Pepto-Bismol and that the baby Jesus looks large enough to captain the high school football team. No wonder Mary needs no urging to Fall on Her Knees ...

There's hockey on the creek and always, a collie dog that runs off with the puck, "Shep! Shep! That'll do!" Taking time from the meal preparation to walk out to the horses and give Old Man Cody his Christmas apple ... Men, cracking nuts and jokes, sharpening the old bone handled carving set ... The turkey, smelling rich, bowls and silver spoons and antique linens gracing the table, gleaming in the candle light ... Stuffing sandwiches at midnight by the light of the open fridge ... So, this is Christmas.

There are honest souls and otherwise. No matter how the chips are stacked against him, the honest horse or pony will do his level best for you. The dishonest one can succeed — but he needs high mileage under knowledgeable hands in order to do so. Just know that when the wheels fall off, as they are wont to do, his default setting is to 'look after number one'.

If you are shopping for children or dealing with adult confidence issues, you need to find the honest horse or pony, no matter how talented the others. It all comes down to character.

Colic frightens me. When one of our young horses was fending off an inexplicable bout earlier this month, all I could think while we walked and waited was this: don't let her be robbed of her chance to do good. In the end, we prayed, the vet toiled and she rallied. It all worked out.

I realized again what it boils down to: Man or beast, making the world a better place is why we are put here. One must not forget.

This excerpt from the *Chicago Sunday Record Herald,* dated 1912, reminds us of those who are at our mercy. May we do no harm and go in peace.

A Horse's Prayer:

Feed me, water and care for me, and when the day's work is done provide me with shelter, a clean dry bed and a stall wide enough for me to lie down in comfort. Talk to me. Your voice means as much to me as the reins.

Pet me sometimes, that I may serve you the more gladly and learn to love you.

Do not jerk the reins and do not whip me going uphill. Never strike, beat or kick me when I do not understand. Give me a chance to understand you. Watch me and if I fail to do your bidding, see that something is not wrong with my harness or my feet. Do not tie my head in an unnatural position or take away my defense against flies by cutting off my tail. Examine my teeth if I do not eat.

And finally, my master, when my youthful strength is gone, do not turn me out to starve or freeze, or sell me to some other owner to be slowly worked to death. But do thou take my life in the kindest way and you will be rewarded here and hereafter. You will not consider me irreverent if I ask this in the name of Him who was born in a stable. Amen.

— Author Unknown

"How can you sell that nice horse? I could never sell a horse like that!"

Here's the thing. Selling a horse or pony that I've grown close to is never easy. Saying goodbye to one that has come to trust me, so that I might trust it, is a recipe for tears, if ever there was one. My reality is that training, then selling my own horses is what allows me to ride.

True confessions? My other reality is that I'm an undisciplined old broad. I have yet to figure out how to make myself enjoy the dodgy horse when there's a better one in the corral. The day I swing my leg over, give a sigh of happiness and feel like I am safely home, is the day my good horse is ready to go on his journey ... and it's the day my next horse steps up to the plate.

If I could change your horsemanship right now, I would say, "Broaden your view".

When riding, it's easy to stick with others of our own ages, abilities and interests. It's a safe approach but it won't enrich our lives as much as if we spend time with seasoned, older riders who have literally seen it all ... younger riders who will instill us with passion, drive and energy to keep us young at heart ... volunteering at therapeutic riding for an understanding of doing our best with what we have and never giving up ... and finally, learning about other disciplines, that we might open our eyes to different brands of horsemanship.

Staying small is easier, yes. It's our choice.

Old horses.

If you are fortunate enough to have one — one that was an extraordinarily good horse in his day — you do not need me telling you that you have a treasure. There is nothing that compares to the sheer joy of settling into the saddle on a horse who has literally seen and done it all. To feel for your stirrup, straighten your rig, then take that happy breath on a horse that is waiting for your next thought. I wish every rider could know, at least once in this life, a horse that delights in solving all problems.

I'm thinking of this as I watch the horses after throwing the morning's hay. There is something about Cody that stops me from turning away and moving on. The others are eating their fill, trading dirty looks, but not him. After a long time at the water trough, drinking long and deep, the twenty something gelding goes off a way then with one hip cocked, just stands there, shunning breakfast.

Hugely high mileage, Cody paid his dues for my son-in-law's family long before I ever knew him. Though we met later on in life, both of our edges somewhat dulled, I have learned to love him for: his little foibles regarding his ear; his zest for apples and cookies; his rage against new horses and an undying love for the ladies; his happy roll of the cricket; his speculative gaze and a jog I could die for. Mostly, I love this horse because he is safe. No matter who is on him, they become invincible, as if they've grown wings.

As I'm watching him, I think of these things and I know, as all horsemen know, that these cannot be mine forever. I am moved to walk up to him, to scratch those well-known places, to lay my hands on his solid body and thank him for all the good he has brought to my life. His eyes acknowledge this.

Will he be here for me tomorrow? I don't know. He's not sick but he's different somehow and when I turn to leave him, I am mindful to say au revoir rather than goodbye.

"I've ridden for years, for most of my life. Lately, there seems to be so much to learn, so much I'm doing wrong. I'm feeling very discouraged." This was part of a message that was sent to me. I saved it because I think that if we're honest, we've all been there.

For many of us, going riding is enough. There are a tortured few of us for whom that will never be enough, that there will always be something more just beyond our grasp, a piece of the puzzle for which we are always searching.

This is good. It's an evolution in our horsemanship. It's the difference between playing the piano with two fingers — pounding out Chopsticks —and making beautiful, soulful music. I only ask that you be patient with your horses and kind to yourself. The exquisite thing about this is that it's a lifelong journey. We will never, ever be done.

NOTES

NOTES

CONCLUSION

HOPE. WELLNESS. LEARNING. REFLECTION.

It comforts me, that I have known and loved these seasons... and that I will know and love them all again.

Writing these stories has been a great pleasure. Some of them have made me laugh in remembrance, while others have brought forgotten tears. Always, being with horses, writing about them, has helped me to learn. I have realized that this thing called horsemanship is a large mirror that shows us about life.

Thank you for finding the time to read *Horse Woman*. I wish each of you a happy trail, wherever it may wind. If something you've seen here resonates, or perhaps you are left with questions, I invite you to become a Keystoner — a Keystone Equine Facebook follower — and send a message to me on this page. We'll hash it out as though we're having coffee at my kitchen table ... because friendship is a vital part of loving horses, too.

FACEBOOK.COM/LIVINGWELLRIDINGBETTER

SUGGESTED BOOK CLUB QUESTIONS

1. Lee's stories reflect a hugely diverse upbringing with horses. What is your experience in horsemanship, so far? How has this shaped your riding and your beliefs? Have your equine encounters had any effect on what methods you most admire and respect?

2. What is it about horsemanship that feeds you? What is it about horsemanship that helps you cope with ordinary life?

3. Lee's stories are not all happy ones. Many times, she writes of regrets, of the horses and people that she has disappointed. What do you regret in your horsemanship journey? If you had the courage and resources to make amends, would you? Which of your riding failures has taught you the most? If you learn from them, are they still failures?

4. Riding horses in public invites both criticism and embarrassment. How have you found a support system or community that encourages you, no matter what? Have you ever found yourself adjusting your riding and beliefs to 'fit in' with a group? Lee writes a story about her reins breaking and buttons popping off her rain-soaked blouse during one public performance. Share your most embarrassing moment, if you dare.

5. Empathy. Hardship. Limits. Consequences. Victory. Loss. What are you hoping horsemanship will teach your children, beyond the usual 'heads up, heels down'? Do you see any advantages that children who ride and know horses have, over others who do not? How can this be nurtured in all children, no matter their circumstances?

6. Lee claims a spiritual connection with certain horses. Have you encountered an equine soul mate? If so, tell us about this horse. How did you recognize that this horse was special?

7. One of Lee's methods is to openly acknowledge fear. Have you faced fear in your riding? If so, when? Have you fully conquered it? If not, how have you adapted to accommodate fear in your horsemanship?

8. How do you fulfill the need to know and touch horses, if they are not a part of your life? If you have long loved horses and are not blessed to be among them, how do you fill this gap? Which of these stories spoke deepest to you, or came closest to feeding your soul?

9. If your group could ask Lee anything arising from *Horse Woman,* what would it be? Assign one of your club members to send her a message on Keystone Equine's Facebook page. Make sure you mention the name of your book club ... and she will answer your question publicly.

INDEX

BECOME A BETTER RIDER
applying the aids	37, 40, 140, 146
being sensitive	39, 74, 92, 125, 138
horse-human relationship	58, 92, 194, 198
professional instruction	35, 46, 69, 139, 158, 179
riding journals	8
self-help	8, 15, 57, 77, 88, 172, 204

BUYING A NEW HORSE
assessing the risk	39, 79, 118
Christmas	192
getting acquainted	15, 39, 81, 155, 185, 192
know thyself	74, 75, 79, 126
naming and renaming	15
professional instruction	158, 198
riding the right horse	26, 43, 62, 90, 201
riding the wrong horse	79, 10
trial rides	12, 39, 118

EQUINE CARE
chiro & body work	73, 74, 83, 88
cold weather	20-24, 29, 31, 33
foot care	88, 196
mares	73, 90, 42
older horses	50, 87, 91, 181, 193, 195, 203
saying goodbye	117, 186
turn out	93, 131, 198
young horses	32, 40, 60, 155

FEAR OF RIDING
admitting fear	75, 81, 85, 197
close calls	49, 117, 145
coming back	35, 47, 72, 75, 80, 84, 197
riding the right horse	43, 84
riding the wrong horse	10, 81, 29, 117
staying safe	33, 40, 49, 72, 85
wrecks	72, 93, 152, 197

KIDS & PONIES
adult involvement	46, 48, 64, 65, 169
expectations & standards	61, 62, 65, 123
loss of interest	11, 64
Rule of Twenty	59, 62
step-up ponies	66, 135

PARENTING A RIDER
ambitious parents	65, 66, 135
instructors	46, 48, 67
looks vs goodness	58, 62
riding the right horse	43, 58

READING YOUR HORSE
confidence	49, 114, 148, 155
crooked & sore	73, 50, 117
expectations & standards	9, 11, 114, 194
mares	73, 78, 90
overdemanding	114, 116, 146
sensitive, anxious horses	6, 59, 60, 74
staying safe	39, 43, 152, 199
turning out	44

TACK & EQUIPMENT TIPS
bitting	59, 136
blanketing	31, 61
cavessons & nosebands	42, 51, 136, 142, 173
maintenance	21, 37, 184, 190
show turnout	33, 137, 186, 188, 193

TRAINING TIPS
arena horses	10, 35, 92, 146, 148, 175
barn sour	44
canter/lope	37, 60, 135, 144, 151, 183
cinchy horses	152, 168
corners	146
doctoring	74, 83, 93, 201
dressage	94, 179
driving	49, 72, 80, 94, 198
gait extensions	37, 42, 51, 89, 94, 146
gait transitions	14, 139, 146, 151
groundwork	34, 40, 50, 167
handling feet & legs	157
herdboundness	32, 38, 120, 121
lungeing	42, 51, 114
mounting	40, 132, 149, 152
moving cattle	87, 171
'natural horsemanship'	167
outside rein	139
overcoming phobias	49, 80-82, 93, 148
parade day	114, 116
pawing	143, 149
'perfect practice'	9, 148
sacking out	92
showing	127-138, 186-189, 193
spooky horses	42, 92, 153, 164
staling on command	24
standing still	40
starting back after a break	33, 93, 155
swishy tails	78, 158
the walk	139, 149
trailering	25, 26, 32, 45
warm-ups	89, 137, 138, 144, 152

LEE McLEAN

Lee McLean owns and operates Keystone Equine in Alberta, Canada. She has earned a reputation for selling well-trained horses and ponies. Such is her confidence and commitment to horse and rider that she guarantees her sales for one year.

She has taught women in the art of riding sidesaddle for over thirty years. From English and Western, to Driving and Sidesaddle, Lee has the prizes—and scars—to prove it.

Lee has a legion of faithful followers on Facebook, a national equine magazine column, and appears at events from small-town horse shows to sidesaddle racing at the Calgary Stampede.

She resides on the family ranch in the Alberta foothills with her husband and a dog.

www.ingramcontent.com/pod-product-compliance
Lightning Source LLC
Chambersburg PA
CBHW060521080526
44586CB00012B/566